To

Au _____ sen

Wh _____ _____

Lydia B_____

Romans 8:28

# THEY LOOKED FOR A CITY

Yente at Seventeen

# They Looked for a City

by

LYDIA BUKSBAZEN

THE FRIENDS OF ISRAEL
Missionary and Relief Society, Inc.

330 Witherspoon Building
Philadelphia 7, Pa.

Dedicated to the Memory of
MY MOTHER

"I thank my God upon every remembrance of you"

Second Edition—1960

Copyright, 1955
The Friends of Israel
Missionary and Relief Society, Inc.

Printed in the United States of America
Library of Congress Catalog Card Number: 55-17705

# Foreword

The writing of this book is the fulfillment of a long-cherished hope to put down on paper the story of my family, from the latter part of the 19th century until the Second World War.

"They Looked for a City" is the saga of a Hebrew Christian family tossed by all kinds of national and personal storms, yet always emerging on the crest of each menacing wave, as if carried by the hand of a merciful God and the force of their faith. It is a pilgrim story of real people whose lives were marked by a two-fold stigma and a two-fold privilege—that of being Jews as well as believers in the Messiah of Israel, Jesus.

The center of this family chronicle is occupied by my beloved mother Yente, because to me she personifies something that is so precious and peculiar—the heart of a Jewish mother, and the impact of her faith upon her family and all those who came in touch with her. She was truly a daughter of Abraham, not merely by physical descent, but by faith also, for like the patriarch of her people, she too "Looked for a City which hath foundations, whose builder and maker is God"—Hebrews 11:10. Her life suffused and permeated by the spirit of her Lord was a blessing to many. It is my sincere hope that the colorful story of her eventful life may continue to bring encouragement and help to all those who will meet with her through the pages of this book.

Now at last Yente has entered the blessed City of her longings, preceded there by her beloved son, my brother Jacob, and followed by her life companion, my father, Benjamin. It is my prayer that those of us who are still on the pilgrim path may in God's own time join them yonder in the City where there are no tears and which is lighted by the presence of Christ our Saviour.

Come, my friend and reader, I will take you into a strange and partly lost world—into Czarist Russia, Poland, and Germany of a past generation, where millions of Jews lived, suffered, dreamed, hoped and perished. Theirs was a fascinating world, steeped in the ancient ways and traditions of the Jew, shaped and fashioned by an ever pressing hostile and sometimes destructive environment.

I will take you to Holland and the people of England, grimly braving the terrors of two world-shattering wars. We shall meet with masses of people and individuals, some kindly, generous, gracious—God's kind of people. And also the others—the hard, the heartless and completely ruthless. Yet all of them have one thing in common. They are not literary fiction, but real people.

The tale of their lives is not spun with the ingenious threads of a fertile imagination, but is real. Here savagery and human brutality meet face to face with Christ-inspired saintliness and the faith which moves mountains and overcomes all obstacles. It is a story stranger than fiction, and I earnestly hope that it will also prove more helpful.

On the background of this colorful canvas is etched the unusual and sometimes breathtaking experience of my own people.

"They Looked for a City" could never have been attempted were it not for the wise and loving help of my dear husband, Victor Buksbazen, who by his unfailing encouragement and with his talents as a writer, helped me continually, editing and correcting each chapter. Much of his own personal and unique knowledge and deep insight into Jewish life, thought, and background have gone into the making of this book.

Here is a testimony of faith which tells in letters spelled out with human lives, the truth which King David, the sweet singer of Israel, once so beautifully described:

> "They that trust in the Lord shall be as mount Zion, which cannot be removed, but abideth for ever" — Psalm 125:1

*Lydia Buksbazen*

# Contents

### Chapter One

## Jakob and Rachel

JAKOB GLASER was a Russian Jew, who, soon after the middle of the 19th century, was kidnapped as a child and conscripted for compulsory military service in the army of the Czars. He served in the Russian army for the greater part of his life, about 25 years. His was an exciting, hard life, colorful but short. Wherever his military duties took him, his delicate devoted young wife Rachel, and his three daughters and son went along with him. The children were born in the living quarters of the divers garrisons of Russia in the Caucasian Mountains. His whole mode of life was that of the typical Russian soldier, even his appearance was that of the Russian. Tall, blonde, blue-eyed, big boned—rather un-Jewish looking. Although living in a Gentile world, he always craved to come back to Jewish environment and to finish his life as a Jew among fellow Jews. A strange fear gripped him that he might become lost to his people and die among strangers. His wife, a devout Jewess, a loving mother and wife, bore the hard unsettled life without complaining; always seeking to bring comfort to her family wherever the army transferred them, but sadly missing the religious life which a pious Jewish woman craves for her husband and family.

Thus it was that Jakob brought his family to the small city of Siedlce, a garrison city, some 50 miles from the capital of Warsaw in Russian Poland. There they settled in a modest home, seeking to take root, weary of traveling, but happy in the thought that now at last their journeys were ended and they could pursue their daily life in an environment which would include worship in the synagogue, instruction for the children, and a day of rest on the Sabbath.

However, they had realized little of their dreams when Jakob, weakened by his many years in the service, became the victim of an epidemic which struck down hundreds. And so the little woman, Rachel Glaser, took over the task of mothering and fathering her four young children.

Her dominant ambition was to teach her son Mottel (short for Mordecai) a trade. More than anything she feared that her boy might follow in his father's footsteps and join the Russian army, and lead the life which had shortened the years of his father. Bravely she struggled to give the children the minimum of education, for in those days education was a luxury only the rich enjoyed.

## Rough Riding Cossacks

At about this time there was a great unrest in Russian Poland. For over a century Poland was ravaged by her powerful neighbors, and divided among the three great empires of the day—Russia, Germany, and Austria. The Poles, always patriotic to the point of self-destruction, again and again rose up against the Russians and her other oppressors. These outbreaks were mercilessly suppressed, with many Poles being killed and thousands deported and sent to the dreaded Siberia. In order to strike terror into the hearts of the Polish rebels and the restless population, the Russian police and the Cossacks were given a free hand. Of course the Jews, as usual, were made the scapegoats of everybody.

The Russians, to divert attention from themselves, incited the Poles against the Jews, according to the ancient recipe—divide and rule. The unhappy and frustrated Poles would vent their spleen on the helpless Jews. Russian inspired pogroms often took place.

Those were the days when the Cossacks, on their swift little fiery horses brought from the Steppes of Siberia, would swoop down like a bolt from the blue, upon the unsuspecting and defenseless people in the streets, swinging their Nahaikas (knotted leather thongs), or using their sabers indiscriminately in the streets of the Polish villages and cities.

A Jew dressed in his traditional long black coat and adorned with side curls, and covered with the velvet cap of the pious Jew, would be a special attraction. Like a hunter at the sight of his quarry, the Cossacks would descend on the Jews, their horses' hoofs trampling down those who happened to be in their path.

## Death Under the Horses' Hoofs

During such a descent of the Cossack detachment upon the Jewish population in Siedlce, Rachel and two of her daughters were caught in the street. Seeing the Cossack rider come upon them, Rachel acted quickly. Throwing herself between her daughters and the Cossack, she bore the brunt of the thong lashes and was kicked on the head by the excited horse. Left bleeding and bruised, the two girls took their mother home, but after weeks of lingering, she finally succumbed to brain injury and ensuing paralysis. Such was the end of this brave and genteel Jewish woman, whose one aim in life was to serve God as best she knew and provide for her family a home and the daily bread.

Sarah was the oldest daughter. She had always been her mother's right hand, taking her mother's place in the home when Rachel was earning a living, and in her mother's work place when Rachel was sick. Quiet, unobtrusive, passionately fond of her two younger sisters and brother, she was the plodder, the realist. Mottel, who came next, had by now finished his apprenticeship in the shoe factory and was ready to go out into the world and earn his own living. Later he married and took his wife and children to South America, an adventure on which so many young married men yearned to embark, but few had the courage or means to achieve.

## Yente With the Golden Hair

The middle girl was Yente, golden haired, fair skinned, blue-eyed, altogether lovely, Yente. She was the pride of the family. Her striking beauty was famous in the little town of Siedlce. And with her beauty went a strong character, and an impelling personality.

She was indeed the sunshine of that little home. In spite of the daily struggle for existence, somehow she always saw the sunny side of life, and would impart to others that rare gift of accepting with a smile whatever came her way, be it joy or sorrow. Yente was an ambitious girl, and like her mother early dreamed dreams of a life without the daily fear of hunger and struggle. She was a hard worker and an outdoor girl.

When the weather was mild, she would prefer sleeping outdoors in the back yard or the neighbor's field, and early in the morning, even before dawn, she would be up, wash herself in the icy cold brook running through the field, and gather wood for the fire and bring water for the household. Life was indeed primitive in those days in Poland, yet looking at Yente, one could see no traces of roughness on her smooth white skin, no sign of fatigue on her fair young face. Her love for children made her the village nurse maid, for whenever she had the opportunity, and they were many, she would take the babies and little children off their mother's hands and go into the woods with them to pick berries and nuts. Then she would return the children to their mothers and be invited to a meal, which she gladly accepted as payment for taking care of them. This would relieve her mother and sister of providing meals for her. At harvest time she would offer her services to the farmers as picker in the fields, giving her again an opportunity to be outdoors and breathe the fresh air, which to her spelled life. Her midday meal would consist chiefly of some bread and milk and some fresh fruit.

The death of her mother, whom she loved above all else, was a blow which brought home to her for the first time the seriousness of life.

The youngest sister, Dora, not yet 10, was wholly dependent upon the support of her sisters.

To Sarah, the eldest, it became more and more apparent as the days went by, that their future was not in the small city of Siedlce. It was unthinkable that the three girls should remain in this garrison city alone, more or less at the mercy of the thousands of soldiers who paraded the streets from early morning until late at night. Sarah felt the responsibility of her sisters weigh heavily upon her, and thus it was that she decided to take them both to the capital city, Warsaw, to seek a living in the ghetto among their own Jewish people. In the big city they would be much safer than in Siedlce, and also have greater opportunities to find employment.

## Chapter Two

# The Big City

I
T was Spring 1896. The great day of their departure from
Siedlce had been decided upon. It was inconceivable to
their neighbors and friends, that the Glaser girls should
actually be packing their few belongings to leave the little
town where they were known and loved by all.

First the friends tried to persuade them to change their
minds, pointing out the dangers besetting young girls ven-
turing out on their own into a city as vast as Warsaw. Some
even said they would share their last crust of bread with
them, if only they would stay on. But Sarah would not be
moved by their pleas.

Her younger sister Yente, by now a blossoming girl of
thirteen and rather mature for her years, was touched by the
concern of neighbors, and above all by the entreaties of her
little friends who loved her dearly. It was hard for her to
part from these children, so precious to her. Then there were
the fields and the orchards, every inch so familiar and precious; and the brook that ran through the neighbor's field
seemed to say, "Stay on, stay on. I'll refresh you, I'll sing
to you and you will be happy here." She had spent many
hours on warm summer nights beside this brook. She had
seen herself as in a mirror as she sat and dangled her
feet in its cool water, refreshing as dew from Heaven—the
brook so peculiarly her own.

She wondered how she could live in the great city where
she heard there were no fields, no wild flowers, and no brook.
She thought of her mother whom she loved so dearly; the
mother who had toiled for her and the others so patiently;
the mother who taught them to fear God and to love Him.
Never again would she nestle in her mother's arms and feel
her stroke her long plaits and hear her say, "My child, it
isn't what man makes that comforts, but what our great God
has given to us that we should enjoy and treasure." Rachel
was a simple but devout woman. She knew God with her
heart. "Children" she would often say, "Remember your
Creator and worship Him. Never be too tired or too busy
to give God His due." That simple creed she instilled into

14

the minds and hearts of her children. Now she was to leave the place where her beloved mother was buried. Would she be unfaithful to her memory by doing so? Never would she have the opportunity to visit the "eternal place," as the Jews call the cemetery, where her father and mother lay asleep, side by side, with the sleep of eternity. She wept at the thought.

For a girl of her age she had great depth of feeling and a wave of loneliness came over her. But her elder sister Sarah insisted and finally prevailed upon her.

## In a Polish Train

At last the day came when sad goodbyes having been said, the three girls took the slow, smoke-belching train, which was to carry them to Warsaw. A tedious journey that was, and seemed endless. The carriages seemed to be filled with peasants and their families, coming from and going to neighborhood towns to dispose of their produce in the market. Several women carried on their backs huge cans of milk, fastened around their shoulders with coarse sheets. Some carried baskets in the crooks of their arms, with eggs and dairy produce or cackling hens. They shared their meals, eating the heavy black bread and smoked garlicky pork sausages at which the Jewish passengers would look askance, and turn away their heads—such abomination!

And they, the Jews, were going to the big city to visit relatives, to buy goods for their small stores, to find work, to see the great rabbis, or to study in famous Talmudic colleges with which the city abounded.

Here and there some who did not have their fare, would hide under the wooden seats in the car, and the women, with their wide skirts, would obligingly cover them up. Poor things, what were they to do? But the conductors were generally up to such tricks and would fish them out. However, ten kopeekes (a dime) would fix the whole matter up, for the time being at least, unless there was a change in the train crew.

Sarah and her sisters looked through the windows as black-soiled fields seemed to run backwards—fields full of promise for a great harvest. The rye was green and luscious and so was the wheat. Potatoes were peeping through the ground, and in between were red clover fields, rich fodder for the horses and cattle.

Here and there the girls would see a peasant cottage with a thatched roof, and the farmers with their barefooted little children, standing in awe before the passing train.

## In the Ghetto of Warsaw

Finally, after many hours, the great Warsaw railway station loomed before them and they stood in amazement. The thrill of the big city held the girls spellbound. The profusion of gas lights in the streets, unknown in the murky and muddy streets of Siedlce; the noise of the horsedrawn doroshkies (cabs) as they rumbled along the cobbled streets on their iron clad wheels; the jingle-jangle of the horse-drawn trolleys; the bulky trucks drawn by heavy-set and big horses; the hustle and bustle of endless crowds, hurrying to their duties, or just sauntering about aimlessly; the big shops with the show windows with a variety of never before seen clothing, and other fancy goods, beyond the wildest dreams of these country girls, awed and numbed their senses. It made them feel lost in this strange and overpowering new world.

Fortunately a friend of Sarah's took them to a small room in the Jewish district, which she had managed to rent for them, after much searching. Now they were in the heart of the Jewish Ghetto, indeed in the very heart of European Jewry. Round about them the streets swarmed with Jews and all of them seemed to be such fine Jews. Most of them wore long black caftans and peculiar little black caps made of cloth, or of shiny black velvet, the headgear of the most pious.

Their faces were adorned with side curls and flowing beards. Their eyes were so sad and dreamy. It seemed the nineteen centuries of suffering and exile looked through their tragic eyes. Here and there one could see a Jew in a great hurry, carrying his "talles," the prayer shawl, and the phylacteries, used during the morning service. He was in a hurry to make minian (a quorum of ten Jews without which there could not be a public service) in the Shul (as the Jews call the Synagogue). Otherwise he would have to pray all by himself, a procedure far less meritorious than partaking in the prayer of a minian. Here and there one could see Jewish boys with their delicately chiseled features accentuated by undernourishment and poverty, their long black coats revealing, as they skipped along boy fashion, the "talles kotten," the four fringed garment with long tassels, the mark of orthodoxy.

It did not take the girls long to realize that here indeed they would feel safer than in the garrison town in Siedlce, where the drunken Russian soldiers and their abusive manner were a nightmare. Surely, thought Yente, her mother would approve of the move they had made, and the thought comforted her. She would work and earn money too.

Sarah already had a job in a furrier's workroom making fur caps, and Yente too would learn. It was Sarah's idea to earn a living for her two younger sisters until they were old enough to learn the trade, but Yente insisted that she wanted to work to help keep them right away. Thus it was that Sarah apprenticed her, strangely enough, to a Gentile furrier. He had several children and Yente was to look after the children part time and learn the trade part time.

This worked out well until pay day, when Yente's boss, an unreliable kind of man, who kept no Sabbath for his Jewish employees, and no Sunday for himself, and who drank away his profits, calmly told his employees they would have to wait for their pay until his next batch of work was completed. This did not suit Sarah at all, and she promptly kept Yente home and bade her "keep house" until a more profitable opening came along. Sarah worked hard, often 16 hours or more a day, and took care of her sisters, watching over them like a mother.

Every week she would bring home some new material for they had very little in the way of clothing. She would sit up for hours, and with the help of Yente sewed for them all, until the time came when they could step out among other girls and not feel too shabby. She even had a high school girl come in twice a week to tutor her sisters, hoping that by so doing they would have greater opportunity to earn a living when the time came. When Yente was fifteen she was working beside Sarah, learning the trade and bringing her earnings into the one room which to them spelled home. Putting together their meager earnings somehow they eked out a living.

In the rush and tear of city life, memories of the past quickly grew dim. The new life crowded out the old. Yente was happy that at last she was able to work and share the burden with her sister. After saving and pinching for many months, Sarah had Yente measured for her first really elegant dress, made by a dressmaker, and her joy was complete.

## A Sabbath Day

The girls always kept the Sabbath as their mother had taught them. On Friday afternoons, the work for the week completed, they would scrub and wash and tidy their home to give it a real Sabbath appearance. The table was decked with a white table cloth, and Sarah, now the head of the family, would kindle the Sabbath lights soon after sunset, just like her mother did before. She would cover her face with the palms of her hands and silently pray a prayer of dedication to the God of Abraham, Isaac and Jacob. She would remember her mother doing it for many years before, when her father still was alive and later in her widowhood, and tears would trickle down through her fingers as she remembered her dear departed.

They would say their short prayers from the prayer book, the part appointed for women on the Sabbath. They had no obligation to go to the Synagogue, for this was a duty and privilege reserved for men who would duly thank God for this privilege, every morning saying, "Blessed art Thou Lord our God Who did not create me as a woman."

The smell of the Sabbath dishes filled the little home. There was "gefilte fish" made of the chopped meat of fresh river fish such as carp, perch, or pike, flavored with a goodly portion of onions, salt, pepper, sugar, and the yoke of egg added to hold it together. They would keep the skin of the fish and then fill it with the prepared fish meat and simmer it in water with vegetables. The fragrance so precious to Jewish nostrils, and indeed to some of the Gentile neighbors, would fill the home and the whole neighborhood on Friday afternoons.

Then there was the chicken prepared in the kosher way, soaked in water for a full hour, and then salted for a half hour, so that no blood would remain in the fowl, for had not God commanded His people to partake of no blood of slaughtered animals?

On the Sabbath table there would be the "Halle," an oval shaped loaf of bread, made with egg and sugar, with a shiny brown crust.

The girls, their prayers ended, their hands washed according to the law of their ancestors, by pouring from a

quart jug three times on a clenched fist, first on the left
hand and then on the right, would wipe their hands, say the
appointed prayer and sit down at the table and give thanks
over the bread, and drink the kiddush wine, the wine of
consecration. Then they would proceed with their meal.
They were happy and proud of their achievement and independence, but mingled with it all was a deep and gnawing
sense of loneliness and sadness in their hearts. Were they not
three orphan girls, trying to put up a brave front in a strange
world?

On high holidays, such as Yom Kippur (the Day of
Atonement), The Passover, and the Feast of Tabernacles,
they would go to the Synagogue to attend the memorial
service, a religious duty in which even women were expected
to have a part.

In the Synagogue they sat in the gallery looking down on
the men-folk beneath, and the cantor who in a highly
cultivated tenor voice would chant the prayers, always facing east. The prayers with their ancient melodies and melan-
cholic dirges would make a profound impression upon the
girls. The candles with their twinkling lights somehow
would remind them of the souls of their beloved departed,
and when the chazen (the cantor) would chant in somber
tones, "El molai rahamim" (Oh, God full of mercy) the
prayer for the departed souls, all the women and some of
the men, would cry aloud, remembering their dead.

On Sabbath afternoons and evenings, or on high holidays,
the girls would go for a walk, as did all the other young
people, promenading along the main thoroughfares of the
Jewish Ghetto in Warsaw, the Nalewki Street. Soon faces
became familiar. Young people greeted one another with a
"Gut Shabes" (Good Sabbath) or "Gut Yomtov" (a good
holiday to you). Friendships would be made and romances
would blossom forth, as in days of old in ancient Jerusalem.
Small groups of friends would go to a nearby cafe for a glass
of tea with lemon and tasty little cakes. If since their last
meat meal six hours had passed, they would have chocolate
with whipped cream, a delight that only the more well-to-do
could afford. But the poorer would indulge at the expense
of the next morning's breakfast.

## The Promenade

The three Glaser girls soon attracted attention not only

because of their regularity on the Sabbath promenade, but
also because a more beautiful girl than Yente could not be
seen. Her fair complexion and long golden braids were the
envy of all the teen agers, many of them vying for a place
to walk beside her, so that they too might attract attention
so richly lavished on her.

It did not take long before some of the young men asked
Sarah for permission to walk out with Yente, but Sarah, a
strict disciplinarian, would rarely approve of that. During
one of their walks the girls had a certain handsome young
man pointed out to them as being a neighbor who was very
quiet and generally kept to himself. He was the son of a
wealthy Jewish cabinet maker, whose shop and work rooms
were within a stone's throw of the girls' home. Some 40 or
more men worked in the shop.

## Benjamin

Yente had often seen this young man and had often admired his quiet but poised manner, and last but not least,
his good looks. He was a refined type of young man, somehow different from the others. When she saw him during the
week, he was generally busy, in and out of his father's factory. He seemed to be self-possessed and she imagined that
he must be very accomplished. His features were regular,
his dark hair and small mustache were always well trimmed.
She often wondered how he found time to keep so well
groomed when he always seemed to be working.

This was Benjamin Sitenhof, the only son of one of the
most respected Jews on Nalewki Street. She wondered
whether he had ever noticed her—probably not. Was not
she just one of the many girls he saw about him day in and
day out? She shrank from meeting him, but it was too late.
A friend of hers introduced him to the Glaser girls.

It was no doubt love at first sight. A friendship quickly
sprang up between them. Yente and Benjamin very soon
knew they would have much opposition from his family, for
was he not the promising and accomplished son of a well-to-
do family, and would not he be able to marry a wealthy girl
from a well-known and honored family? This was the accepted thing in Jewish life. The things that were held in
great respect were learning, wealth, and a good family. By
"good family" generally was meant descent from rabbinical
luminaries and scholars. Matches were arranged by match-

makers who proposed to the parents of each party and would enlarge upon the merits and virtues of the prospective bride and groom, for a consideration, of course.

An accomplished young man would be entitled to a rich dowry, maybe partnership in business with his father-in-law, or, if a scholar he would be entitled to several years of "kest," that is home and board in the in-law's home, until his course of study was completed and the young man was able to provide for the new family.

Benjamin was the apple of his father's eye. At 17 he was not only a master cabinet maker and carpenter, but also the brains of his father's business. He was also a studious young man, diligently studying the Torah and old scholars would congratulate his father upon the accomplishments of his son. Perhaps one day he might even become a rabbi himself and thus bring honor to his father's name. Pampered and idolized by his eldest sister, who mothered him after their mother's death, somehow he remained unspoiled and serious beyond his age.

Now he was confronted with a great problem, such as he had never had to face before. All his needs and all his difficulties were taken care of by a loving father and doting sister. Now he would have to decide for himself. One thing he knew, that come what may, he would marry Yente. Whatever the consequences he felt he could shoulder them. Young and efficient, he felt capable of managing his own affairs. He was thrilled at the thought, that of all his friends, he was the one who won the heart of the most beautiful girl in the whole Jewish area, as Yente was then known. Her sweet nature and natural beauty made a lasting impression on all the people with whom she came in touch. Thirty years later when she returned to visit Warsaw, people still recognized her and cried, "Where are your lovely golden braids, Yente?"

## Benjamin and Yente Elope

It was a shock to Benjamin's father, a venerable old man of good repute in his community, when his beloved son announced that he wished to marry Yente. At first he did not take him seriously, but soon realized that the matter was serious indeed. Benjamin's sister, Sima, flew into a rage and vouched she would have Yente hounded out of town if he did not give up this mad idea. Nothing daunted, Benjamin secretly arranged his wedding in a little town not far from Warsaw.

The small town Rabbi, dressed in full rabbinical regalia, shining black hat with a broad brim, long black coat reaching to the ankles and girded with a black silk sash, presided. Beside the Rabbi and the prospective bride and groom there were only a few witnesses present. The wedding canopy, the so-called hoopa, was erected, and underneath it Benjamin in the presence of the Rabbi, said to Yente, as he slipped the wedding ring on her finger:

"Thou art betrothed unto me according to the law of Moses and Israel." And then added the traditional words which God pronounced concerning His future ransomed bride, Israel:

> "And I will betroth thee unto me for ever; yea, I will betroth thee unto me in righteousness, and in judgment, and in loving-kindness, and in mercies. I will even betroth thee unto me in faithfulness: and thou shalt know the Lord" (Hosea 2:19, 20).

A glass was then broken and the small company shouted "Mazol tov! Mazol tov!"—may you have good luck. Benjamin and Yente were now man and wife, according to the Law of Moses and Israel.

The happiness of the young married people was great, but soon it was to be marred by the insistence of Benjamin's family that their marriage be annulled. Ominous clouds were gathering on their horizon. Yet in all these things there was the hand of God leading through sorrow and tribulation to a deeper and fuller knowledge of Himself, which was to revolutionize their lives.

## Chapter Three

# The Importance of "Yihes"

BENJAMIN'S father and his two sisters vehemently opposed his "misalliance" as they called his marriage. What in the world possessed him to marry Yente! What kind of dowry did she have? Who were her people? All she could show was a pretty face and a pair of golden braids. True, she had a good face, an open face, clear blue eyes and a well-formed chin, that bespoke character and determination.

If she only had "Yihes"—a noble descent of which she could justly be proud. But did she have any illustrious ancestors? Any Rabbis? Any famous scholars? Or at least some outstanding and prosperous merchants? No, she had no "Yihes." All she could boast of was her soldier father, a Jew who almost became a Russian! And she herself was just a country orphan who had to do hard work with her hands to earn a bare living. Let her marry her own kind—not such a fine promising brilliant young man "like our Benjamin."

Of course this attitude did not exactly contribute to the happiness of the married couple. Love does not blossom readily in such soil. Sarah, Yente's elder sister, saw this very clearly and she believed that the young people must get away from Warsaw if their marriage was not to be wrecked on the cliffs and rocks of family disapproval and hostility.

### "Get Thee Out"

Besides, things were not looking too bright for Jews in the Russian Empire in those days, of which Poland was a part at the time. The Cossacks were still riding high, and peasants as well as the town people cunningly incited by the Russian Church and Czarist officialdom, by means of malicious rumors and accusations, were breaking out in riots and bloody pogroms, swallowing up thousands of Jews. There was a wide wave of migration, a desire to get away from Russia and its oppression. Anywhere—the farther the better. Many went to Germany, to France, to England, and above all, to far and fabulous America, the dream of thou-

sands. There the streets, they said, were paved with gold
and all trouble would come to an end as soon as you set foot
in that wonderland.

Sarah felt it her duty to help her sister and brother-in-law,
for after all, what were they but young married children—
she 16 and her groom, 17. Somebody had to take care of
them. So Sarah left for England to prepare the way for
Benjamin and Yente to follow as soon as she would find
work and secure a place for the young couple.

This Sarah did and wonderfully succeeded in her task. For
soon she sent word for the young couple to follow. And so
in the Spring of 1900, Benjamin and Yente left for England
in high hopes for a bright future, not only for themselves,
but also for their first-born, whom they now expected.

Fortunately in those days passports were yet unnecessary.
Only in later years did they become an essential part of
one's being. Man, they said in Russia, consists of three parts
—body, soul, and passport, and the most important of these
was the passport. But in the Spring of 1900 the passport had
not yet become the essential part of his personality.

They journeyed across the Continent of Europe by train,
3rd class, which was hardly a picnic in those days. The
trains were dirty and overcrowded. The passengers consisted of young and old and even babies in their mother's
arms. There was a real Babel of languages and dialects, with
Yiddish more than holding its own. The smoke and coal
cinders drifted in through the doors and windows and added
to the discomfort and weariness of the passengers. All
looked hungry and red-eyed for lack of sleep. A stale odor
of "machorka," a cheap tobacco, and handmade cigarettes,
made the air thick and unbearable. The small compartments
and corridors were crowded with people, leaning against the
windows, eager to catch a glimpse of "Europe" (Russia then
was hardly considered as being European), or sitting on
their bundles or their cheap cardboard and fibre valises.

But this was not an unhappy crowd by any means. Most
of them were young, full of excitement and expectancy.
They were pioneers, about to enter upon new adventure
and to conquer unknown worlds. If one could only pierce
the veil of the future, and know what was going to happen
at the journey's end. Such were the thoughts that pervaded
most of their minds.

What if they were uncomfortable, tired, and hungry;

what did it matter, if at the end of the journey, golden opportunities were to await them, and a new exciting life. Once
and for all they would be far away from hated Russia with
its iniquitous laws, with its corruption, with its maudlin
sentimentality, often changing rapidly into extreme cruelty.
They shall be free; they shall be men among men.

Yente, as always, craved fresh air and open spaces more
than food. So she sat in the corridor for the greater part of
the journey, craning out of the window whenever she could
gain the coveted position. The countryside looked beautiful
and refreshing.

## The White Gates of Heaven

The last lap of the journey, the crossing of the English
Channel, was made by boat. This was the most exciting
experience, as neither Yente nor Benjamin had ever seen the
sea before. What a thrill to breathe in the first whiff of the
salty sea air! To see the endless expanse of the green water,
to hear the mighty roar of the waves beating against the
shore! Oh, the exultation! They could shout for joy! Up the
ramp they came, mingling with the medley of human beings
and their endless bundles, as they eagerly sought to pierce
with their eyes the distant shores of England. At last when
the White Cliffs of Dover came into sight, it semed to Yente
that they were the White Gates of Heaven, beyond which
they would live in unmolested happiness. Here her first
child would be born in a free country. Here even a Jew was
allowed to go about his business without fear of Cossack
lashes and the engineered bloody pogroms of the incited
mobs. Whether knowingly or not, they always looked for
such a city and here it was just within their grasp. O happy
thought!

And then came London. London, the metropolis of
Europe. With awe they stepped out of the train into the
Victoria Station. They fairly caught their breath in amazement at the great luxurious trains and magnificent station
restaurant, of which they just caught a glimpse as they
passed. A new world indeed!

And then there was Sarah! What a reunion! How concerned she was over her "little sister" and how she bom-
barded her with questions. Did she have a good journey? Is
she feeling well? The eyes of the newcomers spoke of their
delight and joyful anticipation. What is an uncomfortable

trip to young people on the threshold of a new happy life?
But little did they know. Fortunately a wise Providence had
not revealed to them the life of wandering, the tribulation,
the joys and the sorrows which they would be called upon
to endure.

## Petticoat Lane

Sarah took them to a small room in Leman Street off
Whitechapel which she had rented for them. She apologized
that it would only be for the time being until they could
find larger quarters and work for Benjamin. But Benjamin
was a master craftsman in his trade and he had no difficulty
at all in finding work as a carpenter.

They lived in the heart of the Jewish section of London.
His work was so near home that he could even drop in for
lunch.

As soon as they had rested from the journey, Sarah took
them to Petticoat Lane, the great shopping street of the
Jewish world. It was the Nalewki Street in Warsaw all over
again, only more so. In shops and on the sidewalks they saw
the crowded stalls displaying everything one could imagine
—all the things precious to the palate and taste of good
Jewish folk. There were the large barrels of salted herring
and pickles, smoked salmon, and black juicy olives, the
aroma of which permeated all the market. What an abundance of fish both from the sea and the rivers!

Near by the little Jew from Lithuania was selling
"beigles," round rolls with holes in the middle. At the top
of his voice he exalted his wares, crying in Yiddish, "Fresh
beigles, fresh beigles, straight from the oven. Refresh your
souls!" Here soul's delight and body's pleasure mingled Jew-
ishly enough into one great harmony.

Near by was a stand full of ties and socks, handkerchiefs
and other white goods and haberdashery. Also a stall loaded
with remnants of beautiful colored materials. Its owner
was shouting as he displayed his multicolored wares, "Pick
'em up, pick 'em up. Dress like a queen for next to nothing."

There was a little cripple who hovered over a barrel of
miscellaneous stockings, watching feverishly the dozen or
so pairs of hands which dived down into his "store" to match
up a pair. If you found the matching stocking all you had to
pay was three pence. With an eagle's eye he watched the
hands lest one pair disappear without payment. When asked

to help match a pair, he would shout back, "Tomorrow, tomorrow, come back tomorrow." This would bring forth a howl of laughter from the crowd as they knew his unchanging retort. Then there were the shops and stalls full of new and old clothing and yard materials. What wonderful bargains for the poorer people both Jew and Gentile!

Yente stood as if hypnotized. The manner of these Jews was the same, and yet so different from those she had left behind in Poland. The same features, the same faces, and yet strangely different. Bondage fell away, and an atmosphere of freedom pervaded the very air. She felt at home among these people. Tears of joy came to her eyes as she thought with a prayer of thankfulness in her heart, how privileged she was to have her first child born in this blessed country. Her first born would be British!

In the distance Big Ben was booming out an evening hour and near-by chimes answered with a joyful harmonious chorus of high, clinging, ringing tones.

Her sister Sarah worked hard and insisted on paying the rent so that Benjamin's earnings could be saved up for the anticipated doctor's fees and considerable expenses connected with the coming of a baby. Evenings would be spent in their modest little room and they would enjoy the twilight atmosphere while it lasted. When night came they would often sit in the dark, either lacking or trying to save the pennies necessary for the gas meter. They would sit and talk about the life back home in the old country, but already it seemed to be fading into the past, crowded out and submerged by this new exciting life in the great throbbing metropolis of the world.

## The Tempest

Yente was happy. But was Benjamin? Of late a change had come over him and he would often sit silently and ponder. How could Yente know what was going on in the mind of her young husband? How could she know that in his thoughts he was back in his father's spacious home, the pride of his family, where his every wish was acceded to almost before expressed. The truth was that life in London was not at all rosy. The little room in Leman Street was dingy and depressing. The cooking odors of all the other tenants blended into one nauseating smell, from which he often would withdraw and take a walk in the wide street of Whitechapel, where he could at least breathe freely. A sixth sense warned her that her happiness was imperiled.

Yente would accompany him as long as possible because she felt the lack of fresh air even more than Benjamin, but neither would tell the other their innermost thoughts for fear of making the other unhappy. After all Benjamin was only a boy, suddenly brought face to face with the duties and burdens of manhood, burdens frightening and heavy for his slender shoulders.

In the evening Sarah would come and sit with Yente while Benjamin was out on his walks. As time went on it seemed that Benjamin's walks would grow longer and longer. Anxious for her sister's welfare, one evening Sarah decided to follow him. She saw Benjamin entering a house in the neighborhood and after a while as she waited, she recognized him as he came out in the company of two other people. To her amazement they were Benjamin's elder sister Regina and her husband. Now Sarah could piece things together. She knew that Regina was planning to go to America, and now in all probability she stopped over on the way to the United States. But why had not Benjamin told them about her arrival? Why the secrecy? She felt hurt and disappointed in him for the first time, and then fear gripped her heart. There must be a plot, something was going on. They still wanted to part Benjamin from her beloved sister and maybe take him away to America, or perhaps send him back to Poland.

A fearful premonition held her rooted to the spot. How could she tell her sister? But how could she keep it from her? Her baby was expected any day now and surely he would not listen to his sister at such a time. But Sarah heard that Regina and her husband were heartless people and known as trouble makers.

She went back to their little room, and when she arrived out of breath, to her surprise she saw a small group of people standing near the entrance. What had happened in her absence? Quickly she made her way through the crowd, her heart pounding with fear. She realized the doctor and the midwife were there. The baby had arrived. And she? She was not even at her sister's side when she needed her most.

And where was Benjamin? Did nobody know? Sarah sent a neighbor to the address from which she had just returned and soon Benjamin came.

Mazol-Tov Daddy! What a fine daughter you have Benjamin! What are you going to call her? Elizabeth? Sounds a little unJewish, but it's all right! Come to think of it, isn't Elizabeth the slightly disfigured English for the good Hebrew name, Elisheva? "The Lord has promised on oath." Of course it is! Now He kept His promise! Blessed be His name!

Sarah was so glad that she did not have an opportunity to tell Yente of her distressing discovery. Now she would keep it to herself and save Yente any anxiety which might upset her and the newborn infant.

## Chapter Four

# Forsaken

WITH the birth of baby Elizabeth a more adequate home became an urgent necessity. Benjamin did not earn enough as yet to make this possible, so as soon as Yente received her strength, Sarah decided to accept a position with a wealthy Jewish fish merchant as nursemaid to his children.

It was a good position, but it necessitated her living out of town away from her sister. But then the distance was not so terribly great and they arranged to see each other on her free days.

Yente was left alone. In the few months of their stay in London, Benjamin had picked up a little English, but Yente had very little opportunity of hearing English. Yiddish was predominant in the neighborhood and certainly in the market down Petticoat Lane. Hitherto Sarah had done most of the purchasing for the little family, but now it was up to Yente to take over the complete run of the home. Benjamin worked at his trade of cabinet making and brought home his meager earnings, barely sufficient for their rent and food.

And then something happened which changed the whole course of their lives. Little Betty was only five weeks old, when one night Benjamin did not come home. Yente sat up waiting for him into the wee hours, but he did not come. She knew nothing about his sister and her designs for him. In the morning she looked about the room and something told her to go through their few belongings. In the drawer of the bureau in a corner, she found an envelope which she hastily opened. It was a note in an unfamiliar handwriting. It was from Regina, Benjamin's sister, telling Yente that her husband was on his way back to his father in Poland, and that she better forget him. Enclosed were three pound notes ($15.00) for her immediate needs. Yente was stunned. She read and reread the note. No, it could not be true! She must be dreaming. Surely Benjamin would not do such a thing! Why he loved her and their baby, and had promised never to leave them. She refused to believe it.

But the bitter fact was that Benjamin did not come home. Slowly, against her will, she had to believe that after all it must be true. Her heart was torn in agony. The baby whimpered asking to be fed.

Feverish thoughts raced through her head. She had to take action. Her mind was made up. She fed the baby, tidied the room, dressed herself and her little one, and went out. Her face was flushed and her heart beat wildly. But there was determination in her eyes. If Benjamin was on his way to Poland, so must she be. She must get her papers together —her marriage license, that was all she needed. She looked for it, but that too was gone. Inexperienced and young as she was, she realized that something dreadful had happened. She broke down and cried without restraint.

The most valuable possessions she had were the feather beds made of goose down, which she brought all the way from Poland. She would sell them and if that was not enough she would also sell her wedding ring. Carefully and with a broken heart she took off her wedding ring for the first time and put it in her purse.

She asked a neighbor to keep an eye on her baby, and took her feather beds under her arms and made her way to the Lane, where she was sure she could sell them. Sure enough, a ready buyer came along who offered her the handsome sum of five pounds. To Yente this was a little fortune, even though the down was worth much more. But it meant an open door to her husband, to the father of her child. She did not stop to think why Benjamin had done this to her or to rebuke him. All she knew was that she must go to him, that somehow his sister must have hypnotized him and succeeded in sending him home.

## Robbed

Carefully she placed the five pounds together with the three she already had, and put the purse in the pocket on her hip and hurried home to her baby. Now she would take the baby and go to the railroad station to find out how much the fare would be, and if necessary would also sell her wedding ring. But she must, before anything else, find someone to interpret for her in the travel office. Her English was still so limited and hard to understand.

With the baby in her arms she arrived in the Lane. Instinctively she touched her pocket to make sure she had her purse, and to her horror she found it was gone. She was robbed! Robbed of all her possessions! She reeled and screamed. People came running. The world seemed to spin around her, and then she felt strong arms upholding her, and a voice as if in the distance asking "Who is she?" People said, "She says she has been robbed. But robbed of what? She is so young and beautiful. Whose baby is she carrying?" On and on went the questions. And then a husky man, dressed in a navy blue suit leaned over and steadied her. She clutched at the man's sleeve frantically, and through her tears cried, "It is gone, my purse, all I had, my feathers, my all". He looked at her and could not understand. She was talking Yiddish. People were eager to interpret the girl's frantic explanations. Now he understood.

He was a policeman, one of those big burly and kindly men, a Bobby, she and Benjamin had so often admired. What a difference between this policeman and the Russian back home. She was sure he would help her. He would find her purse for her. How could anybody be so cruel to her and her baby. People took her into the store. An empty box was turned with the bottom up and she was made to sit on it. "Calm yourself" they advised her, "and tell us what happened". Yes, she must be calm, she must be strong, she must clear her mind, to tell them of the two-fold tragedy which had befallen her.

She told of her husband. They glanced at the finger of her left hand. She told them the ring was in her purse which was stolen, as she had decided to sell anything to get back to her Benjamin. And where was her marriage certificate, they asked. Oh, yes, she could explain that too. Her husband took it with him. And then the crowd looked at one another and at her knowingly.

There was a hushed silence. What a pathetic figure, and such a story. The policeman obtained the translated story. He asked if she knew anybody in London. Indeed she did. She had a sister, but did not know her address. Oh, what was happening to her, she thought. These were strangers to her. How could they understand what had happened to her in such a short time. What she told them seemed so incredible, so fantastic. People murmured. It was obvious their credulity was strained to the limit and their sympathy was ebbing out fast. People began to walk away slowly.

Abraham Sitenhof, Benjamin's father, believed in "Yihes"

Mr. and Mrs. Benjamin Sitenhof and Baby Elizabeth (Around 1900)

Left to right: Jack, Mary, Elizabeth (standing), Lydia (now Mrs. Buksbazen, the author), Yente Sitenhof, and son Ernest. Around the year 1913.

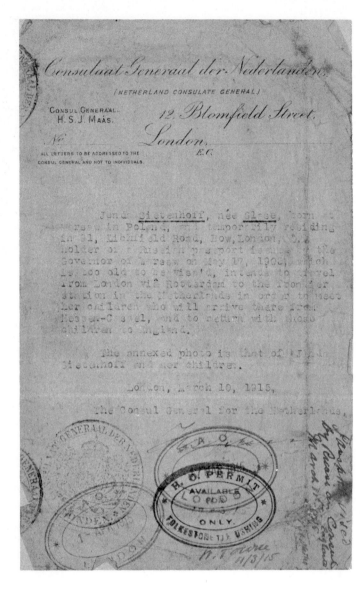

Yente's traveling document

## "Sons of Mercy"

Then out of the crowd a little man appeared. He talked quickly, heatedly, and asked "Can we Jews, who call ourselves 'Sons of Mercy' allow this girl to be stranded with her baby in a strange country? What does it matter whether we believe her story or not. The fact is that she is in distress. I call upon you, everyone of you to rally around her. Isn't she a daughter of Israel in anguish? She needs our help. Have mercy, have pity". His words acted like magic. Already he was passing around an old battered hat. The crowd increased. Excited whispering filled the air, and hands were stretched out. They were now willing hands, helping hands. The hat went around and around until it was full, and then the policeman took it and placed his own contribution in it. Tears were in the eyes of many.

Here girl, daughter of Israel! Here is your fare. We cannot find the despicable person who robbed you, but we believe you and we will see that you join your husband, if indeed you have one.

And now a voice came from the back of the large store. Some one whispered, "It is Mr. Chaim Rosen himself." "Daughter", he said, "did you say you had a sister Sarah who was a nurse maid out of town?" "Yes, yes", she cried excitedly. "Her name is Sarah Glaser". "Come, my child", reaching for her hand. "Your sister is with us in Hyams Park. She told us about you and intended to write you this week. Come, I will take you to her." A miracle had happened. This was the wealthy fish merchant. The crowd looked on in amazement. The baby began to whimper. The little man who started the collection now beamed with satisfaction and triumph.

Through her tears Yente smiled. The sun was shining for her again, even through heavy clouds. Soon she would see her Sarah and soon, God willing, she would see Benjamin again. In her heart a prayer went up to God for the care He took of her. In her heart she knew all would be well again. How bighearted were her Jewish people. Just like in Warsaw. Always ready to help one another from the fullness of their hearts. She felt so grateful and proud.

Mr. Rosen was a kind man. He took Yente and her baby out to his home to meet Sarah. When they arrived his family welcomed her as if she were their own daughter. Sarah's joy was great to have her beloved sister with her and to be able to take care of her needs.

For two months Yente enjoyed the hospitality of this friendly Jewish family, as nobody would as much as listen to Yente and let her take the long journey, until she had fully recovered from her shock and the baby was old enough to travel.

The country home of the Rosen family stood all alone in the woods in beautiful surroundings. They kept their own chickens and a cow. Once again Yente tasted the joy of country life, and though her heart was yearning to be with her husband in Poland, she enjoyed every moment in the peaceful surroundings and among kind people.

## The Homeward Trek

It was at the time of the Coronation of King Edward VII that Sarah took Yente and the baby back to London, to see her off at Charing Cross Station for the Continent, across the English Channel. The sight of the jubilant, joyful masses, shouting and hailing their newly-crowned king, made the two young women only more conscious of their own loneliness and helplessness. The hearts of the sisters were heavy as they parted. Sarah took care of all her sister's needs and provided clothing, some food, and many little things, which she hoped would insure a comfortable journey. Yet having no identification papers, not even a birth certificate, Yente and her baby were delayed several times on the way. This was an unforeseen circumstance which caused her to run out of clothing for the baby. Soon all diapers were used up and there were no facilities for washing them on the way. Herself, she could stand everything, the squalor, the weariness and the hunger. But her poor baby! She nursed her as best she could, and was as careful with her pennies as possible.

Exhausted and weary, she felt the strain increasingly of sitting on hard benches with a three months' old baby in her arms. Oftentimes she would go without sleep whole nights. The long tedious trek brought them to the Russian border. The German train crew left and the Russians took over. So far the trains had been anything but clean, although the Germans did come in once a day to sweep up, but from now on the part of the journey through Russian Poland became unbearable. The Russians contended that since she was without papers she and her baby were public charges and treated her accordingly. One night during one of the numerous train changes, Yente was hustled into a dark section of the train. Before she realized what was happening she was pushed inside a compartment with her baby, and told to sit on the floor. The baby was uncomfortable and irritable. She herself was on the verge of tears.

Suddenly out of the darkness of the compartment in a corner someone was moving. She was rooted to the spot, and then a terrible laughter rang out, the laughter of a maniac. She tried to scream but no sound would come. She tried to laugh, but she was paralyzed with fear. Again that laughter, hideous and frightening. Panic gripped her and then she screamed. Thumping at the door behind her with one hand, she feverishly groped for the handle. The door was flung open from the other side. In a flash the conductor took in the whole situation. The guard had made a mistake and put her in a compartment with a drunken man. Now everybody was distressed and ashamed. How could such a thing have happened? The conductor was infuriated and full of apology. He led her into his own compartment and tried his best to quiet little Elizabeth, who by now was screaming at the top of her voice.

Warm milk was brought for mother and baby which calmed their nerves. They brought her warm water to wash the grime off her face and to tidy up her baby. A kind Jewish passenger who was on his way to Warsaw offered to help. Realizing the child's needs, he dashed out at the next station and somehow managed to return with a clean sheet, which he promptly tore apart to provide the necessary diapers.

The tedious and long journey lasted another six seemingly endless days. Would they ever arrive in Warsaw? At every little village station they stopped. But by now word had been passed from place to place, that a lone Jewish mother with a baby in her arms was on her way. And so whole delegations from the towns and villages, oftentimes headed by the Rabbi, would come to the station to greet the beautiful Jewish young mother and her child. They would comfort her and bring her a hot meal or other necessities.

## Reunion and Forgiveness

At last they arrived in Warsaw. Yente hardly expected Benjamin to be at the station upon her arrival, but Sarah had cabled him, and, what a joyful surprise! There he was waiting for her. He told her he had been meeting every incoming train for the last six days, his anxiety for her safety and their baby increasing from day to day.

Now, thank God, they were united again, and no one would ever come between them. They were two young people in love. Everything was forgotten and forgiven. Shamefacedly Benjamin told her how his sister had prevailed on him to return, and how in a weak moment he had given in at last, but how dreadfully he had suffered ever since. He had learned his bitter lesson and vowed never again would any of his relatives influence him in his decisions. And how true he was to these vows!

Yente was happy again. Happy as the day is long. At first, grudgingly her father-in-law accepted her, seeing how determined his son was to stick to his wife. But soon admiration and a hardly concealed pride became visible in his attitude toward his daughter-in-law. For where was a braver girl in all of Poland? To face her misfortunes so courageously! The family now were reconciled. In any case, Yente's sunny nature could not bear grudges for long. Peace was restored.

Yet this peace was to be shattered by an awesome discovery, destined to change their lives and that of generations yet unborn. For one day Benjamin came face to face with his Messiah.

## Chapter Five

# Benjamin Meets the Messiah

FOR a while the sun was shining bright and benign upon the lives of the reunited family. Little Elizabeth was the joy of her father's heart. She resembled him to a striking degree with her dark curly hair and small regular features, and whenever he had the opportunity he would spend a few minutes admiring her, for she was as beautiful as a doll. When Elizabeth was two, her baby brother, Ernest, was born. There was great rejoicing at the birth of a son. To Yente life seemed to be crowned with happiness. Often she would thank God in her heart for all His wondrous love to her. For her to look up to God with gratitude was as natural as her sunny "Good morning" to the workmen as they filed into the factory every morning. Many a time she would be there to take a hot dinner to her Benjamin or her father-in-law. The factory was working full time and over. Her father-in-law's business was flourishing, and altogether Yente was the envy of many a young lady and young mother with whom she came into contact.

The only thing which marred her happiness was the poverty round about her in the Jewish Ghetto. How some of these poor Jewish men and women struggled to eke out a living! It reminded her of her own former home, her widowed mother and the years of struggle, and at such times she would cling in a childlike way to Benjamin, fearful lest something should come along and destroy the happiness which she was experiencing and enjoying to the full.

Benjamin carried on his work in his father's carpenter shop, turning out beautiful pieces of furniture, for he seemed to be gifted with his hands beyond measure. "Golden hands" they used to say concerning him. He could do anything with them. There was a skilfulness and sensitivity about them that evoked the admiration of many. Soon the young man, scarcely twenty years old, became the foreman of his father's large factory, and there was no doubt that he would later become partner and eventually the heir of that prosperous establishment.

But the Lord has a way of dealing differently than human expectations. He had better plans for young Benjamin than turning out good furniture. His was to be the job of being a fellow worker with The Master Carpenter of Nazareth in helping to mold souls through the power of the Gospel. But on this peaceful summer day, when a Catholic customer came into the shop, Benjamin had no way of knowing about that.

The customer had a small book in his hand with black covers, and he handed it to the young foreman with the words: "Here read this. Some missionary gave it to me. It seems to be a religious book, but it does not have the approval of my church, so I must not read it. Perhaps you would like to read it".

## "That Name"

It proved to be a copy of the New Testament in Polish, forbidden not only to the Gentile customer, but above all to an orthodox Jew. Benjamin had heard about the book in a very vague manner ever since he was a child. It was connected with the unmentionable name of "That Man". They called him by the cryptic name "Yeshu", interpreted to mean: "May his name and memory be blotted out". Strange and terrible things concerning "That Name" and those who believed in him came to his mind. They were all haters of the Jews, he thought. In olden days they used to put the Jews to the sword. They massacred and persecuted his people, and even now few of them had a kind word for the Jew. All the fearful wrongs, injustices, and degradations which his people suffered were graven deep into his soul. His was the memory of a persecuted people.

When he thought of "That Name", he had visions of crowds in the streets, oozing a strange and frightening religious fervor. They carried graven images and painted pictures of a Woman with a Baby in her arms, and those of others supposed to be saints, things that were an abomination to the Jewish mind. The crowds were singing strange songs, the very sound of which made his soul shudder. He knew that whenever such processions passed in the streets, it was the part of wisdom for a Jew to disappear from the street, because those who did not, often were victims of uncontrollable outbursts of religious fervor, and of mass psychosis, ending with split heads and black eyes.

Is it any wonder that Benjamin was confused upon receiving this book. And yet he was eager to know more about

Him, to understand the personality Who had evoked so much fervor and faith, and seemed to have a limitless sway over these masses. Stealthily he put the book in his pocket, determined to read it in privacy. In the silence of his own chamber he began to study the book. He expected to read burning words, full of denunciation and hatred for the Jews, but he found nothing of the kind. Indeed it was full of sweetness and beauty. It was the story of one Whose life was inexpressibly beautiful, and His death so cruel and undeserved. The more he read, the more he was fascinated by the book.

When he read the Sermon on the Mount tears welled up in his eyes. It opened a new world of love, beauty, and holiness, unmatched and unsurpassed by anything he had ever read or heard. He went through the Gospels and continued reading the other books of the New Testament and the Spirit of God was working within his heart. He felt more and more drawn to the amazing man of Nazareth. Surely He was a man of God.

The more he read the precious New Testament, the more convicted he became of sin in his life, and the need of a Messiah. He read and reread the whole New Testament until he became very familiar with its pages. There was no question that this must be the true Messiah for whom he had yearned since childhood. This yearning he inherited from past generations, uncounted and forgotten, but reaching back through the centuries and millenniums to the dim days of the ancient history of his people.

## The Living Dead

For a long time he wrestled within his heart. He sought light and the Lord heard the longing of his heart. Gradually it grew upon him with an unshakeable conviction that He was beyond any shadow of doubt the Messiah, the very Son of God, foretold of prophets, longed for and prayed for by his ancestors even until the present day. He could do no other than accept Him.

This, however, was more easily said than done. What about his father, what about his friends, and what would his young wife, Yente, say? Would they call him a traitor, or think him to be just plain crazy? They would hound him out of town. They would give him up for dead and sit Shuva, that is, mourn over him as if he were dead. A candle would be lit in the room; all mirrors would be veiled in black; his father would take off his shoes and sit in his stockinged feet upon a low footstool with that fixed stare of utter despair which is worse than the mourning after one who died. To them he would be a living dead. Nobody would dare mention his name to his father or to any of his loved ones. They would deny him altogether and act as if they had never had a son or a brother. His own beloved Yente would forsake him. At this thought he felt a sword thrust at his very heart.

It was a burden so crushing for a young man scarcely out of his boyhood that he felt he could not face it at all. But then there was the irresistible Christ appealing to him and calling him all the while: "And every one that hath forsaken houses, or brethren, or sisters, or father, or mother, or wife, or children, or lands, for my name's sake, shall receive a hundredfold, and shall inherit everlasting life". He quoted the words which he had read on a number of occasions in that little black book. But now these words seemed as though they came from the mouth of the One who was crucified for him, Benjamin. His look was a challenge. It was full of sadness but also pleading. He could not endure it any longer. He would confess Him, come what may. He would pay the price, no matter what it be.

Yente noticed one day how Benjamin would sit for hours reading out of the little black book, and wondered what it was that was so utterly engrossing him, but she said never a word, knowing that one day he would of his own accord speak to her about it. To Benjamin the New Testament was the greatest revelation of his life. He now understood so much that had been a mystery to him before.

After Benjamin's conversion his whole life changed. His own family noticed the change. He was quieter and more subdued. He could not conceal the change in his life. It was too vital a part of his being. For months he went about his business with a far away look in his eyes. People commented on it and some even thought he was losing interest in the business. Little did they know of what went on in his young mind and heart. To him a new world had opened, new light and understanding. The time came when he could retain his new found joy in the Messiah of Israel no longer, and after a great inner struggle, he went to his father first, to tell him of the great light which had come into his life.

## "I Have Come to Bring a Sword—Not Peace"

Then the worst of Benjamin's fears came true. His father at first thought him to have become mentally unbalanced. He tried to talk him out of this "strange delusion". But Benjamin was adamant. He quoted prophecies from the Old Testament, pointing out that they were fulfilled literally in the life of Jesus. They were so numerous and accurate in detail that there was no possibility of mistake. Besides he knew in his own heart that He was the One for whom he had always longed. Finally his father gave up arguing, and gave up Benjamin for lost.

He would have to leave home and right soon, and he, Abraham, would have to forget he ever had an only son, upon whom all his hopes for the future were centered. He wished his son were dead, rather than see him become a Meshumed—an apostate.

With a heavy heart Benjamin went to his wife, trying to convey to her his newly found faith. But she too, always trusting, faithful, and understanding, she too turned on him. No, this was the last straw. She would certainly not live with a Meshumed. He would have to choose between her and his Jesus. All right, if he cared more for Him, more than for his wife and family, he could have Him, but she would stay right here in Warsaw with her two babies.

Heavy hearted and burdened with a crushing weight, Benjamin decided to leave his loved ones. Deep in his heart he believed that some day when their wrath was over and tempers cooled, he might be able to be reconciled to his loved ones and reunited with his family.

But now he must leave his homeland. And whither could a young man go when the 20th century was in its infancy, but to America, that golden land of opportunity for all men? Yes, that's where he would go!

Soon he was on his way to the land across the ocean. After a night of misery and sleeplessness in the third class train compartment, he found himself red-eyed weary, and infinitely sad, in the city of Kassel, Germany. Here he would have to spend about six hours waiting for his next train to take him to the port city of Rotterdam. Lonely and discomfited he thought he would go and see one of the Rabbis, of whom he had heard previously, and thus kill the dragging hours of waiting for his connection. On the street he asked a passerby for directions to this Rabbi, whose name he knew, and directions were promptly given to him. When he arrived at the address, it did not take him long to find out that he was in the home of an evangelist, who, by some strange coincidence or predetermination, bore the exact name of the Rabbi. This evangelist became to young Benjamin what Ananias was to Paul after his experience on the road to Damascus.

# Chapter Six

# A Strange Prayer
# Strangely Answered

Benjamin was shown into Mr. Ludwig Sommer's study, a somber thickly carpeted dimly lighted room, the atmosphere of the solid brown furniture and book-lined walls, embracing him warmly. There was a hushed quiet over all, which seemed to permeate Benjamin's weary body and to relax his perturbed soul. The dignity and yet friendliness in the room beckoned him to enter and be still.

Had the maid who opened the door to him not said that Herr Prediger Sommer (Preacher Sommer) would see him in a few minutes? What did that mean? Benjamin did not know much German, but sufficient to understand that this wasn't the home of a Rabbi, but of a Christian preacher. Why, he had only prayed on his arrival at the Kassel Station, that the Lord would open up the way for him and make His will plain, and here was the answer already!

"Before they call, I will answer; and while they are yet speaking, I will hear"—these were the words Benjamin had read in the Scriptures recently, and here he was experiencing just that. What a wonderful Saviour to have as a friend, thought Benjamin, as he sat in the leather chair opposite the large oak desk. What would the Prediger look like, he wondered? Would he be surprised to see a Jew? Would he be welcome? He wondered what attitude believers in Jesus, other than Roman Catholics, took toward a Jew. That much was sure in his mind, that a true believer in the Jewish Messiah could never hate or persecute the Jew, and how wonderful it would be to meet such a Gentile Christian.

The door opened, and there stood the Prediger. For a brief moment Benjamin caught his breath! The stately figure in the doorway, dressed in a Prince Albert cutaway with a broad cravat covering his chest, came forward with slow deliberate steps, a warm smile of greeting on his striking bearded face. He was a man in his fifties, tall, upright, with a wealth of white hair, his well groomed white beard accentuating his aristocratic bearing. But the most distinguished feature about him was his friendly twinkling blue eyes, which seemed to speak to you even before he opened his mouth. To Benjamin in that brief moment he embodied all the outward features of his newly found Messiah, as he visualized Him, and immediately he shook his hand he knew here was a friend.

After formally introducing himself, the Prediger asked what he could do for Benjamin. On explaining as best he could in his broken German, how he came to be there and begging to be excused for the error (for which he secretly was thankful) the preacher said calmly, "Benjamin Sitenhof, I have waited for you, yea I have even prayed for you. I perceive you are an Eastern Jew from Poland. I have always yearned to have the opportunity to witness to just such an Israelite as you, and the Lord in whom I believe, has sent you to me." Whereupon Benjamin burst out with the story of his recent conversion. Oh, how he too had longed for just such an opportunity, to tell someone who would understand, someone who would rejoice with him. And here was the very man. He unburdened his heart amid tears of joy and relief, and this man whose very presence radiated warm comfort, listened enraptured. He opened his arms to him as a father and for the first time since his conversion, Benjamin knelt with his newly found spiritual father to pray and thank God for all His ways and tender mercies.

## To Eat or Not To Eat

As they rose to their feet a lady entered the room. Joyfully the preacher introduced Benjamin to Mrs. Sommer who welcomed him warmly. Dressed in black with white trim at neck and cuffs, her face, serene and kind, she talked quietly and gently to young Benjamin, like a mother to her son. Taking in the whole situation in detail so quickly, Benjamin was surprised when she suggested that he be their guest for the evening meal.

Never before in his life had he eaten in the home of a Gentile. Would they serve pork of some kind? Ancient taboos inherited from long forgotten generations still exerted a powerful influence on his thoughts and feelings. It was easier for Benjamin's soul to accept the Lord Jesus as his Saviour than for his stomach to be reconciled with things unclean. Without knowing, his soul was echoing back the feelings of another Jew who followed Christ but who still objected to things unclean. "Lord . . . I have never eaten anything that is common or unclean" cried out Peter. Even so did Benjamin's soul object to that sudden departure from ancient tradition. Besides this, the hour was getting late. He had not had a real meal for many hours and had been so absorbed that he forgot about food. He looked at his watch. In two hours his train would leave for Rotterdam. Oh, how he longed to tarry here with these loving people. As if reading his thoughts, the preacher ventured to suggest that he stay over night and leave on the same train the next day.

And if their dear guest objected to eating meat which was not Kosher, surely "Mutter" as he called Mrs. Sommer, would find plenty of other food acceptable to their visitor. Benjamin's misgivings gave way rapidly before this onslaught of great kindness and Christian hospitality, and without further coaxing he readily agreed to stay over night with his newly-found friends.

That meal was a memorable one for Benjamin. This was his first taste of Christian friendship. Never in his life had he experienced such a wealth of sympathy and understanding, and from strangers at that. What miracles faith in Christ could achieve, he thought. To think that here were complete strangers to him, people he had never seen or spoken to before, and yet here he was talking to them after two hours as if he had known them all his life. Was the tie that bound them together, the bond of the Jewish Messiah, so strong and deep that it could blot out all else? Even the fact that he was a strange Jew from Poland in the home of a German Gentile, who had nothing in common with him in the ordinary sense? And so the deep joy of spiritual oneness and Christian fellowship in the Lord was Benjamin's portion that night. Now he understood the fervor and zeal which only faith in a living Saviour could impart. That night he had a strange and wonderful peace in his soul.

By noon next day it was evident to Benjamin, and also the preacher, that he would change his plans and postpone his journey to the States. All that morning Benjamin had been eagerly questioning Prediger Sommer concerning the Scriptures. There was so much that was not clear to him. He wanted to have all explained to him. He wanted to delve deep into the treasures of the Word. And so it was that his newly-found friend invited him to stay in his home for a few weeks, when they could study the Scriptures together. This invitation Benjamin eagerly accepted. Nothing was important to him now, all he wanted was to feast on the treasures of the New Testament and here was God's servant—a man conversant with it all and willing to spend time with him to expound and study the Word. It seemed too good to be true.

In his great enthusiasm he almost forgot he had a wife and was the father of two children. He was simply in love with his Lord and Saviour, and was so anxious to know him better, that all else was secondary in his thoughts. And this same zeal and desire stayed with Benjamin for the rest of his life. Always he put the Lord first, even though the cost was very great at times.

And so for weeks he sat at the feet of his great teacher, learning and satisfying his hungry soul. His spiritual growth in those weeks was remarkable. The Sommers had two sons about his own age and they were soon fast friends. And always the Prediger would say wistfully, "I prayed for an Israelite and the Lord sent him to me". Oh, how he loved Israel! Benjamin loved his teacher and looked into his face reverently as he expounded the Scriptures to him, sometimes scarcely believing that he was anything less than an angel from Heaven.

### "Call Him Jacob—Letter Follows"

Benjamin had written to Yente when he decided to stay with the Sommers, but had no reply. He wrote again and again, and then one day a telegram came announcing the birth of their third child—a second boy! This brought Benjamin down to earth, as it were, and overjoyed, he wired Yente, "Call him Jacob—letter follows".

He knew that his instructions that his newly-born son should be called Jacob would greatly please Yente and that for two reasons. Yente's father, of whom she had a very dim but fond memory, was called Jakob and she wanted to perpetuate his memory by calling his grandson Jacob. Then, too, the fact that Benjamin was willing to have his son named Jacob and not some outlandish Gentile-sounding name, was evidence to her that he had not broken with his people and that the bonds of love for his own were in no way affected by his newly-found faith in Jesus the Messiah. This stratagem of love was not without success.

There ensued a lively correspondence between Yente and Benjamin—a tug of war—Yente imploring Benjamin to return, and Benjamin begging Yente to join him. He tried to convey to her the satisfaction and joy his newly-found Messiah had given him. He told her he had only just started to really live, and how much he wanted to share that life with her. Yente was eager to see Benjamin and show him their new baby. What a lovely big boy he was, and how she longed for Benjamin to again take his rightful place in the family as the father and bread winner. She had missed him and sorrowed after him more than anyone could understand, but she had kept her sorrow to herself. Somehow she hoped that in time she would win Benjamin back to Judaism.

With that thought growing in her mind, she one day ventured to broach the forbidden subject to her father-in-law. Instead of chiding her, he encouraged Yente to go alone if necessary, leaving the children with a nurse. But Yente would not hear of it. She would take her three precious children with her wherever she went.

So the day arrived when Yente, packed and ready for the journey to Kassel, said her goodbyes. Most of all she was sorry to leave her father-in-law whom she had learned to love. She would miss him and he would be unhappy without her. Her ever smiling face and dancing blue eyes were as a tonic to the old man, even when she teased him and made him hold the baby while she attended to something trivial. He would look at her wistfully and ask, "How long, sweet Yente, how long will you be here to be the sunshine of my life?"

He knew that sooner or later Yente would have to join his son who was lost to him, and in his heart of hearts he hoped that she might be the one to win him back to Judaism. He made sure that Yente and the children were well clothed and had new linen and bedding to take along, these being the first essentials of a new home. There were the down and feather beds (he bought the best for her), the pillows, and sheets, and tablecloths. He provided the best luggage he could get, and as a parting gift he presented a pair of silver candlesticks to Yente, making her promise to be sure to use them every Friday night at dusk.

Little Elizabeth, now four, and Ernest two, held tightly to each other's hands while the baby of six weeks slept in his mother's arms. Little did Yente think as she entered the Warsaw Railway Station, accompanied by her father-in-law and other members of the family, that this would be her last

glimpse of Warsaw for many years to come. Little did she
know what a great change was about to take place in her
young life and with that change, years of toil, tears and suffering, but for all that they would be years of happiness in
her newly found Messiah.

## Yente Comes to Kassel

Benjamin, overjoyed when he heard that Yente and the
children were coming, went about as in a dream. He roamed
the old part of the town through the narrow crooked streets,
the houses of which dated back to the 17th century, to find
a suitable home for his family, and with the help and
recommendation of the Prediger, he rented a three-roomed
furnished apartment in the basement of a picturesque ga-
bled house, which he knew would appeal to his young wife.
The money which he had on arrival in Kassel was carefully
budgeted for immediate needs. Prediger Sommer not only
preached, but he owned a fine religious book store and print-
ing plant, which he ran with the help of his sons, and there
too Benjamin was welcomed to work, at least temporarily, to
earn his keep. Thus his dear friend looked after him not only
spiritually but materially as well.

Benjamin loved to walk through the beautiful old city and
over the old bridge which spanned the river Fulda meander-
ing through the town. He would stand and gaze into the
murky water dreaming of the time when "someone" would
stand beside him. Then as he made his way home through
the adjoining park he would wonder how long it would be
before Yente too accepted the Messiah Jesus. For of that he
was sure, that sooner or later she would see the light and
share his new happiness. He prayed earnestly that this might
take place soon after Yente's arrival.

Then the day arrived! It was a warm June afternoon when
he made his way across the vast Friedrichsplatz to the station. The market was in full swing. The neat rows of stalls
displayed anything from tempting country butter and eggs
to men's and women's clothing. Children darted in and out
of the rows. There was luscious fruit and the tempting aroma
of ripe plums greeted his nostrils. He stopped just long e-
nough to buy a pound of cherries, which were irresistible,
and which would make the children happy on arrival.

The train stopped with a jerk and getting little Elizabeth
to hold on to one side of her voluminous skirt, and Ernest

on the other side, and holding Jacob in her arms, Yente
made her way to the carriage door. Before she even got a
glimpse of the platform, Benjamin had seen her and hastened
to open the door to help her out with the children. The reunion was warm and hearty. Before the warmth of their deep
love for one another the memories of estrangement and mis-
understanding melted away like snow in the rays of an
April sun. Benjamin looked fondly and not without pride
upon his comely wife and bewildered children, taking in for
the first time this strange new world. Yente and Benjamin
had so much to tell each other, but that must wait till later.

The great Friedrich Station awed Yente, and the children
clung close to her side as they made their way to the exit.
So many elegant horse-drawn cabs were busy picking up
and discharging passengers, it was a fascinating scene, and
it reminded Yente of their arrival in London, England, just
four years ago. Having rounded up the luggage, Benjamin
proceeded to one of those elegant cabs, and Yente was
thrilled as a child at the prospect of riding through town in
such a grand conveyance. The little "droschkes" with their
ironclad wheels which used to rumble with such deafening
roar along the cobbled streets of Warsaw, were really no
comparison to these fashionable cabs, with rubber tires running smoothly along the well paved asphalt streets of Kassel.
The drivers with their little derby hats with a colored feather
were a sight to behold. The horses were so well groomed and
impatient to be off. At last having loaded luggage and family, they were on their way.

Yente had not even thought about where they would live.
But Benjamin had a surprise for her. They rode through the
beautiful Koenig Strasse and Yente felt like a queen on display with her family. When they arrived at their apartment,
the modest little home held Yente spellbound. Like a new
bride she admired everything, running from one room to
the other—her happiness unbounded. It took so little to
make Yente happy thought Benjamin. What a lovely nature
she had. Everything pleased her and she missed nothing in
the apartment. The children in bed, Benjamin and Yente
had their supper, and talked till late into the night. There
was much to ask on both sides, and neither of them broached
the subject of Benjamin's faith that night. They were so
happy to be together again. To Yente's keen eye, however,
even that first day she noticed a change in Benjamin. He was

different! Tonight she told herself, she would not even try to find out why. She was tired and she would look at him through different eyes tomorrow. Of one thing she was sure, that she had done the right thing to come to him.

Yente must have been very tired for when she awoke it was broad daylight and for a moment she wondered whether she was dreaming. Then it all came back to her, memories of the day before, and with a start she jumped up remembering the baby would need attention, and that little Elizabeth and Ernest would be hungry. To her amazement, on opening the door to the kitchen she found them seated around the table, dressed and washed, and eating breakfast. Benjamin sat beside them, his eyes beaming at his little offspring and telling them little stories while they ate. There was such complete happiness in that scene. Yente was almost sorry she had opened the door. What a different man Benjamin was! In Warsaw he would never have done such a thing. How kind and considerate he had become. What a gentle manner he had with the children. What had he read in that little black book to change him so? She dressed hastily, promising herself to watch him carefully all day. After they had eaten breakfast, Benjamin took Elizabeth and Ernest for a walk.

## The Battle for a Soul

This would give Yente time to clear up. She took stock, while she did so, of the apartment and thanked God as always for His blessing in bringing her and her husband together again. Benjamin had said something at breakfast about how quickly the Lord answers prayer, and had added: "How I wish you knew Him too, Yente dear". His words came back to her now. What did he mean? To whom was Benjamin referring? No doubt to "that man". Could it be possible that Benjamin knew something about Him that she had never heard? She would question him on his return and try to find out more about this mystery which had changed her husband so completely.

Benjamin only waited for an opportunity to tell Yente what the Lord Jesus Christ meant to him. How completely changed he was—"Born again of the spirit", he said, and what a deep joy he was experiencing in the knowledge of his Messiah. Yente listened bewildered, trying to formulate some kind of an answer which would be effective in bring-

ing Benjamin back to the fold of Judaism. But how could
she, a woman, stand up to Benjamin who knew the Old Testament and the Talmud so well, and could quote from it,
while she could not even open her mouth. For in Judaism
religion as it concerns the Scriptures and the Talmud was
only for men, and women were not well instructed.

All she was taught was to say a few prayers. In the morning upon getting up she would recite "Moide Ani"—"I thank
thee O Lord, Oh Eternal and living King that thou didst
restore my soul to me after a night's rest". She also knew that
every Jewish person when in grave danger must exclaim
"Shema Israel". "Hear O Israel, the Lord thy God is one
Lord". Upon the saying of which any ghost or ghoul was
sure to vanish. She knew that on Sabbath eves she must kindle the lights and covering her face with both hands, silently offer a prayer, beginning with the words "O God of Abraham, Isaac, and Jacob". She knew all about keeping her food
Kosher, that she must prepare her meat by soaking it an
hour in water and then salting it thickly with salt; so that
not a drop of blood might remain in the meat. She still remembered how her Gentile neighbor used to sneer at her
whenever she did that and say, "You are washing all the
goodness out of your meat". But she never took any notice
of her. What does a Gentile woman know about things Jewish anyway?

And many other things Yente knew pertaining to wifely
and motherly duties of a true loyal daughter of Israel. Of
Christians, she knew that they worshipped images and hated
the Jews. How was she, poor unlearned Yente, to answer
the profound arguments from the Holy Book which seemed
to prove that "J"—no she would not even mention the name
—was the Messiah after all.

She was dumbfounded. Benjamin kept quoting Isaiah 53
right from their Hebrew Bible, not even from the "little
black book," the New Testament. He said if any Jew with
an open and unprejudiced mind would read that chapter,
which was omitted in the synagogues whenever the Old
Testament was recited, and would then read the circumstances of the birth of Christ in the New Testament, he
would not fail to see that Jesus was the promised Messiah
whom the Jews rejected and many Gentiles accepted.

These words stayed with Yente. Day by day they would
ring in her ears, and she could not help linking Benjamin's

changed life to this belief of his. If only her father-in-law were here she thought, he could surely give Benjamin the right answers and win him back to Judaism. Again and again she marvelled at Benjamin's calm manner and the joyful way he lived.

## "The Strange Phenomenon A Gentile Who Loves the Jew"

Benjamin was anxious to introduce Yente to his good friends Prediger Sommer and his family, about whom he had told her so much. This indeed was a different world, thought Yente. They were such refined cultured people, and yet so modest and kind. They put on no airs and there was a radiance and peace in them which Yente longed for deep in her heart. And above all, the Prediger had told her how he and his family loved Israel. "But why," she asked, "when the whole world hates the Jew?" He explained to her so gently that he could not help loving the Jews because he loved the greatest Jew of all, the Messiah Jesus Christ, who was foretold by the Jewish Prophets. This was all so new to Yente. She pondered all these things in her heart.

Meanwhile her Benjamin kept pointing out to her that only Jesus is the Messiah of the Jews, and that the prophecies of old became real only when fitted and joined together in one Life—His Life. Who else but Jesus could be the servant of God spoken of in Isaiah 53? And Yeshaia (Isaiah) surely was a good Jewish Prophet, not a Gentile, or even a Christian. "Benjamin", said Yente perplexed, "I am only an unlearned woman and you are a scholar. I cannot answer your arguments, but I am sure there must be an answer and I am going to find it. Oh, if only your own father were here he would know what to say to you. But I will find the right answer, come what may."

One day, being unable to find any peace, she decided to get the Jewish view on the whole question. She would go to the local Rabbi and ask him to explain Isaiah 53 to her.

## The Rabbi is Annoyed

Soon after she had reached this decision she called on the Rabbi one evening. He admitted her rather unwillingly. Rabbis never seemed to have time to talk to women, she thought—they were always so absorbed in their world of learning.

She told him who she was and in her natural frank manner came right to the point. "Rabbi", she said, "I must ask you a very important question. I want you to explain to me the 53d chapter of Isaiah the Prophet. Tell me to whom does it refer. 'He is brought as a lamb to the slaughter'? Explain this chapter to me please".

The Rabbi was stunned. How dare a Jewish woman come to him with such a request! He half expected her to ask one of those perennial questions that Rabbis are asked by good pious Jewish women, like, what is one to do if a drop of milk by mistake is spilled into the chicken pot? Must she get rid of the chicken, or is there any way whereby the Rabbi could circumvent this painful and expensive necessity? Or, perhaps she would ask him concerning some question pertaining to the ritual purity of women. There were so many fine points of the law and often the pious women were perplexed to know what was the right and God-pleasing thing to do.

Those religious questions, known as "Shoales" were commonplace for a Rabbi. With that he was prepared to deal swiftly and with final authority, for just a trifling consideration. But here was a woman, "Eine Ost Juedin", a Jewess from Eastern Europe, daring to propound a question that has perplexed the great minds of Jewry from times immemorial. And the dispute is by no means solved. Some say that Isaiah referred to the Messiah. Others that he meant the Jews who are always the inerrant sufferers and the victims of the Goim. Meantime the Christians are making capital of this mysterious and baffling prophecy claiming that "that man" is the one of whom the great prophet spoke. And here is a simple woman confronting him with that puzzle. He thought of the old proverb, "A fool can throw a stone into the garden, which ten wise men will not be able to remove". He put her in her place.

He cut her short, ignoring her pleading look. "Woman," he said sternly, "religion is not for the woman but for the man. Go about your household tasks, forget what you have heard, keep your dishes Kosher and look after your children and your husband. That is all that is expected of you," he added. With that he showed her the door and ushered her out, slamming the door behind her. Yente could scarcely regain her breath. Her mind was in confusion as she stood outside the door. This was surely not the way to answer a woman's simple question. What had she said? What had she done to so enrage the Rabbi? What a difference in his manner to that of Pediger Sommer, the Gentile! Why wouldn't the Rabbi answer a simple question pertaining to the Jewish Scriptures?

## "Out of the Depths"

With tears of humiliation and resentment streaming down her face she made her way home. In the dark she groped her way quietly to her door and turned the key in the lock. The children were asleep and Benjamin was at one of the religious meetings he attended so often, from which he would return so happy and elated, that sometimes she almost caught that joy herself. She went to her bedroom in the dark. And suddenly for the first time in her life, she felt impelled to fall on her knees and cry out: "Oh God, if Isaiah 53 speaks of the Messiah and Jesus Christ is the one who fulfills this prophecy, then forgive my unbelief and have mercy upon me. Oh God, give me a sign that He indeed is my Messiah. Leave me not in uncertainty," she cried in the agony of her soul. And then Yente heard, as from afar, a voice, and saw an angel filling the dark room with a strange light. And the voice said, "Daughter of Israel, be assured it is the Messiah Jesus Christ of whom the Prophet speaks. Believe and be saved". Her vision faded, and as she rose from her knees she knew that her spiritual rebirth had taken place in that hour.

# Chapter Seven

# "Jerusalem" in Hamburg

TO Benjamin, the fact of Yente's sudden miraculous conversion meant joy complete. He had not dared to hope, even in the secret places of his heart, that his newly found Messiah could work so quickly. This surely again proved to him beyond a shadow of a doubt that through the Messiah Jesus, all was possible. To him, who loved the truth and had diligently sought after it, it was painful to think that He who was the Truth and became flesh, had been rejected and was being rejected by Israel. The blindness and prejudice of his Jewish brethren appalled him, and when he had thought about Yente and that she too could not see the Truth, his heart had ached and he had cried to God "with a loud voice" for the light to shine into her life. He knew that nothing short of a miracle could give Yente that spiritual experience which he had, and which had so changed his life completely. And that very miracle had taken place! Oh! how he praised the Lord!

One day Mr. Sommer told him that a Hebrew Christian pastor and missionary, Dr. Arnold Frank of Hamburg, would be in Kassel and he wanted Benjamin to meet him. Benjamin had already heard about Dr. Frank, who even in those days, was known as the father of Hebrew Christians in Europe, and about whose hospital and mission called "Jerusalem" in that great city of Hamburg, Benjamin had heard so much.

It was there that thousands of Jews from Eastern Europe discovered Jesus as the Messiah of their fondest hopes and prayers. It was in "Jerusalem" of that great Hanseatic city that thousands of Jews found a home, when the doors of their ancestral homes were slammed in their faces, because they dared confess "that man" as their Redeemer.

Dr. Frank invited Benjamin and Yente to come to Hamburg for baptism, and so the young couple with their three children were duly baptized by Dr. Frank in the Hamburg "Jerusalemkirche".

A new life opened up to them, a life made completely happy through the knowledge of the Lord Jesus Christ as their Saviour. Though they were "babes in Christ", they were

55

healthy babies, with that constant hunger for "the food that perisheth not." No wonder they were growing fast in knowledge and in the faith.

Benjamin had an older sister Dora, who years ago had married a business man, David Fogel, from Odessa in Southern Russia, and moved to Westphalia in Germany. As children they had understood each other and Dora, although older, had always looked upon Benjamin as the pride of the family, the one who knew the Torah and the "hope" of the family. Her sudden departure for Germany had always puzzled Benjamin. How anxious he was now to meet her again and tell her his "good news". Then one day his long anticipated hope came true. But imagine his amazement, when on entering her home the first thing upon which his eyes rested was a New Testament text which hung on the wall—"Jesus said, I am the Light of the World." Puzzled, he asked his sister the meaning of that in her home. And then the story came out.

## Vision on the Mount of Olives

Many years ago, Aaron Fogel, a Jewish merchant of Odessa, and the father of David, Benjamin's brother-in-law, came under the spell of a remarkable man by the name of Joseph Rabbinowitz, a prominent lawyer and Jewish leader in Bessarabia, Southern Russia.

It was at the time when suffering drove many Jews to desperation and to a frantic search for refuge. Jewish blood was flowing freely in the streets of Kishineff, the home of Rabbinowitz.

Burdened with the plight of his people, Rabbinowitz went to Palestine to see what prospects there might be for establishing a colony for his persecuted brothers in Russia. When he arrived in Jerusalem, he was shocked to perceive the sad condition, both materially and spiritually, of the Jews whom he met there. They were mostly old people who came to die in the Holy Land—not to live—disheartened, without hope and vision, and living on charity sent to them by pious Jews in Europe, or else indulging in peddling in the streets of Jerusalem.

The land was devastated, lifeless, and poverty stricken beyond description. No, Palestine at that time did not look like a solution for the Jewish tragedy. Disheartened and discouraged, he decided to go home and to tell his people to look elsewhere for shelter, as the time of their return to Palestine had not yet come. In all probability they would have to wait until Messiah comes; and as to that, who knows when it might happen. Perhaps today, perhaps tomorrow, in a year, or, perish the thought, never at all!

Heavyhearted he decided to walk up the slopes of the Mount of Olives to cast a last glimpse upon Jerusalem, so precious, so desirable in exile and in lands afar, but so disappointing when encountered face to face.

In silent meditation he sat down on a stone. In his mind he went quickly over the history of his people. The call of Abraham, God's promises to him and to his children; Egypt and the oppression there; then back again, brought by the mighty hand of God under Moses through God's grace and bounty; disobedience and rebellion on the part of his people; prophets and seers, kings and leaders sent of God, only to be disobeyed and rejected; and that man of Nazareth, of whom he once read secretly in a little Hebrew Testament; those amazing words which somehow never escaped him, "O Jerusalem, Jerusalem, thou that killest the prophets, and stonest them which are sent unto thee, how often would I have gathered thy children together, even as a hen gathereth her chickens under her wings, and ye would not!"

(Matthew 23:37).

And in a moment of sudden illumination like the prophets of old, an inexorable conviction came to him—

"The key to the Holy Land and to the future of Israel is in the hands of our Brother, Jesus!"

This sudden persuasion shook him to the very core of his being, and with this thought burning in his soul, he went back to his native Bessarabia in Russia, and in flaming words, borne on the wings of a great faith and enthusiasm, he preached Jesus, Israel's Messiah and Saviour. Joseph Rabbinowitz continued to identify himself with his Jewish people and saw the need of bringing Christ into the Jewish synagogue, home, and street.

As a result of his fiery testimony, his own wife and his seven children, as well as hundreds of other Jews of his own city and of neighboring Odessa, and many towns and villages, accepted Christ. Thousands of Jews in Southern Russia, for the first time in their lives were compelled to give serious thought to the claims of the Messiahship of their Brother, Jesus.

Aaron Fogel was among the first fruits of Rabbinowitz' labor. When his son David married Dora Sitenhof, neither of them were as yet believers in Jesus. Soon they left for Germany where they established themselves in business. But then Father Aaron arrived from Russia to visit the young Fogels. And so full was he of his great Saviour and the wonderful Gospel which he heard, that soon both David and Dora also accepted Jesus as their Lord. This happened a-round the year 1900.

Thus God amazingly led brother and sister, by devious ways, one in Poland and the other in Germany, to find Christ, and in finding Him, also one another.

In the few years since the conversion of David and his family, he had preached the Gospel to Jew and Gentile alike, using every available hour to witness for his Saviour. David was a very successful business man, a man of character and resolve. He was highly respected both in the community and at the chapel where the family worshipped. David was a man of rigid discipline and courageous action. He was most zealous for the faith and preached Christ whenever possible. His vacations were invariably spent holding evangelistic services in different parts of Germany. Benjamin's sister, Dora, was of small stature, but with a great heart, a loving and gentle nature and a ministering angel to all who knew her.

## Salesman for the Lord

The evening before Benjamin's departure, he confided in his brother-in-law and his sister his great longing and aspiration that he might be called of the Lord to be a full-time missionary to his own people. That was his goal, and he told them that all his strivings would be to that end. David promised to try and help him achieve his aim. "In the meantime," he said, "let us work together and grow together." Benjamin did not understand what David meant until he told him his plan. Benjamin would travel for David's company, and during his journeys to all the important cities of Germany, he would have many opportunities of witnessing for the Lord. This appealed to Benjamin immediately and he arranged to start at once.

What a surprise for Yente when Benjamin returned to Kassel with the news of David's and Dora's conversion, and a new shiny black bag containing samples for his new position. Benjamin a salesman! Benjamin was a craftsman, a master cabinet maker, but no salesman! Yente knew that, but seeing his enthusiasm she said nothing and rejoiced with him. She had great faith, and even as a young believer she knew that God could make of Benjamin what He wanted him to be. Her love for her newly-found Messiah was unbounded, and together they were happy in the assurance that they could endure all things.

Little did they know how soon they would experience the "valley of the shadow."

## Chapter Eight

# The Beauty of Holiness

WHEN their fourth child, a bonnie fair girl, came along, they named her Marie Hannah after their good friend Mrs. Sommer, upon whom they looked as their spiritual mother. To the Sommers, Benjamin, Yente and their children were as precious as their own, and never would a season of rejoicing or a holiday go by without the two families spending it together at the Sommer's home in that beautiful suburb called Wilhelmshoehe.

Here Benjamin saw the treasure of the Christian life displayed in all its loveliness. Here he learned the beauty of daily family devotions. Here he had an example of the spiritual riches which await the believer when he dedicates his life wholly to the Lord. How he longed to do just that.

Together the two families would go to the beautiful park at Wilhelmshoehe. Together they would climb the white stone steps leading to the crystal clear fountains and ponds beneath the monument containing large gold fish, much to the delight of the children. This was their favorite outing.

On public holidays when there were crowds gathered to enjoy the beauty of the scenery and to inhale the fragrance of the tall age-old trees, Benjamin would produce a batch of tracts and distribute them to the crowd. Many times he would enter into conversations with individuals, explaining to them the way of salvation. Benjamin was happy at such times. It was here that he obtained his very first experiences as a witness for His Master. On many occasions he would join some of the other brethren and take part in open air meetings. Thus he grew in the knowledge of the Lord and the Scriptures.

The prayer meetings which were held at the Chapel twice a week were faithfully attended by Benjamin, and whenever Yente could leave the children asleep, she too would creep out and join him at the Chapel.

## A Dread Disease

Yente tried as far as possible to relieve Benjamin of the family problems and burdens. But she could see that his work was taxing his strength. He was beginning to look wan and thin. In her heart she was filled with anxiety lest he should become ill. And Yente was not the only one who had noticed Benjamin's pale face, for Brother Sommer too was aware that Benjamin's health was not as before, and he mentioned this to Dr. Schmidt, a believer keenly interested in the Sitenhof family.

One evening after prayer meeting Dr. Schmidt approached Benjamin on the subject and made an appointment to see him the next day. It was then discovered that Benjamin had one lung seriously affected by the dreaded tuberculosis and that immediate treatment was imperative at a sanatorium.

It must be borne in mind that tuberculosis in the early years of the century was one of the most sinister diseases which seldom let its victims off without exacting the supreme penalty. There were no modern medicines like penicillin and streptomycin or any of the life-saving mediums. Early discovery of the malady, good nourishment, and fresh air, were the only hope of the one afflicted.

Yente tried to be brave when she heard this sudden turn of events. Before her conversion she would probably have broken down under the impact of the bad news, but now she bore up bravely. She carried her burden to the Lord in prayer daily drawing strength from the fountain of living water. David was notified immediately, and after consultation with the doctor it was arranged that Benjamin go to the sanatorium at Liebspringen in the Rhineland, famed for beneficial results in similar cases. There it was hoped the disease could be checked.

And so it came to pass in February of 1908 that David found a small home for Yente in the city of Biebrich am Rhein so she could be near Benjamin, realizing that it might take months or even a year until he could be discharged.

David was indeed like a father to Yente and her children. He lost no time and counted not the cost in getting the little family settled. Although he had two children himself, he divided his time between taking care of his own and Yente's family.

As for Yente she was at her best in times of trial. Hidden resources of strength, courage and faith welled up in her when the storms of life seemed ready to overwhelm her. Now added to her natural qualities of spirit was her strong faith in her wonderful Messiah, who promised her personally never to leave nor to forsake her.

## "A Woman of Valor"

Yente, as always, full of initiative, knew that she could not leave the whole burden on David's shoulders, so she went to work looking for suitable employment which she could do in her home to help feed her children. Some days she would take in sewing, alterations and similar work. At times she would leave the two older children at school and the two younger at a neighbor's and do a day's housework at the home of some Christian friend.

She had found a Chapel to which she attached herself at once, for to Yente spiritual food meant as much as physical. Somehow in spite of all her burdens and thronging duties, she managed to attend at least the prayer meetings after putting the children to sleep. The Christian friends tried to help her. They were impressed with the courage and determination of this Jewess who loved her Lord with a zeal which put some of them to shame. How she worked, day and night to keep her little family clean and well fed. And she was expecting yet another little one!

Benjamin's heart too was heavy when he was first told of his condition. Who would take care of his little flock, he pondered. But seeing the way Yente took hold and observing her courage and faith, his faith too was strengthened. He let the Lord take over and he responded favorably to the treatment. After the first few months hope for a complete recovery was beckoning.

Yente's days were full to the brim. She washed and shopped and cooked and ironed for her own family and then for others. She seemed to have superhuman strength. She was hardly 26 and looked younger. The Lord's favor was plainly written in her lovely face. Baffled by angry waves she was calm and serene, mistress of her boat and its precious little crew, their course set by the Star of Hope.

## A Stranger at the Door

One evening when she had put the children to bed and was mending some clothes, there was a timid knock at her door. At first she thought she had imagined it, for who could be coming to see her at that time of night. It was already 8:30 o'clock and she knew of nobody who might call on her that evening. However, on hearing the knock a second time she went to the door and as was her wont, peered through the small round glass peephole in the door to see who was there. Without opening the door she asked who it was, and there came to her vision a bearded man of medium stature.

A pair of tired eyes met hers. Then came the reply, not in German but in Russian, "Pojalooista, otvoreetye dver!" (Please open the door). She opened the door without another thought, and asked the stranger to enter. Who was he, she demanded, and whence did he come? He sat down and breathed heavily. "My name is Herman Berg," he explained, "and I come from the city of Kiev in the Ukraine."

Then he unfolded a story of woe, very much along the pattern of suffering and tragedy common among the Jews of Czarist Russia. Unable to stand the gross injustice and persecution of his people, he joined some underground movement against the Czar. Then he was caught and pressed into the service of the Czar as a soldier. But in the Russian army his lot was even worse. For apart from the hardship of a Russian soldier his lot was singled out for special ridicule as a Jew.

Nothing he did would satisfy those over him. "Jid, Jid" (Jew, Jew) was the derisive cry that followed him wherever he went. He decided to run away from Russia, even though his heart was breaking for his wife and two children left behind. But what chance would he or his family have if he stayed on? Abroad he might be able to improve his position and eventually deliver his wife and children from the plight of the Jews in Russia.

And so he made his way across the border, risking imprisonment and Siberia. Eventually he arrived in Kassel. Only this evening when he came out from the railroad station looking bewildered for some place to go, "Herr Maximilian" the cab driver who was waiting for a passenger, noticed the strange and confused Jew and directed him to "Frau Sitenhof." And here he was. Could she please help him? Yente knew Max, as they called him in the chapel, for he was a Christian and highly respected among the brethren.

The stranger could speak no German but she noticed that he was a man of refinement and culture. He was only about 30 years old, and well spoken. His face was kind, though sad, and his small black beard and friendly eyes made a favorable impression.

He was an experienced mechanic, he told her, and he was

sure he could earn a living if only he could get a job to repair sewing machines and things like that.

But what was Yente to do? How could she, of all people, herself so badly in need, help another one without a roof over his head? And that someone could not even speak the German language. And then she was a lonely woman with little children. Something must be done, and that fast, for the evening was already far spent. The first need was a place to let the weary wanderer rest his head. As for the future, she could talk to her Lord in the stillness of the night and ask Him for guidance.

In a few words she told him about herself and her position. Her husband Benjamin was sick with tuberculosis in a sanatorium and they had little children to care for. Nevertheless, she ended cheerfully, I have a source of comfort and support of which you know nothing. And then she told him of the Messiah of Israel and how she had learned to lean heavily on Him regardless of difficulties and problems.

He listened intently without a word. But when she finished he said: "I too need a fountain where I can draw strength and wisdom and comfort. Will you please tell me more about it tomorrow?"

That night Herman Berg spent at the Salvation Army shelter to which Yente directed him. Yielded completely to His will the Lord was willing to use her to help this lost soul.

Bright and early next morning he turned up at her home. He looked a different man, rested and clear-eyed. Yente found a room for him nearby and then they surveyed the situation together. She promised to help him all she could for he needed her tongue to interpret for him. In the evening they went to the chapel to prayer meeting, and although Mr. Berg could not understand what was said, the quiet hour of meditation and reverence impressed him more than anything else. He was so grateful when Yente translated to him the sense of the meeting.

### Gentiles with a Difference

Never in his life had he met such strange people. True, they were Gentiles, but so different from the ones he knew back in Russia.

> "Oi, Oi, Oi,
> Shikker is a goy
> Shikker is er trinken muss er
> Weil er is a goy"

Lowenburg Castle in Kassel.—Wilhelms Hoehe

Lydia—Sweet Sixteen

Victor at twenty-two

Yente was fond of her grandson
John, Lydia's firstborn

Front row: Bride and groom,
Lydia and Victor Buksbazen. Back:
Lydia's parents, Yente and
Benjamin Sitenhof.

Yente and Benjamin befriending
a little refugee boy from Germany

The author's sons at ages seven
and eleven, Victor, Jr., and John
David

("Oi, Oi, Oi
Drunk is a goy (Gentile)
Drunk is he and drink must he
'Cause he is a goy . ")

Thus the Jewish boys and girls would mock among themselves the drunkenness and the debauchery of the Russian
Gentiles. It gave them a little taste of vengeance and a
pleasing sense of their own superiority. But these people,
though Gentiles, were different. They were reverent, med-
itative and possessed of a peace and serenity which appealed
to him greatly. "Could it be," he mused, "that that Jesus of
whom Mrs. Sitenhof spoke had something to do with their
strange behaviour?"

## Yente's First Trophy

Yente introduced him to the brethren and Max assured
her that he would help him find a job or part-time work.
There were others who were eager to help, and prayer was
offered for this lonely Jew who had been thrust in their
midst and who seemed so keen to understand all that went
on. But weeks went by and due to his inability to speak
German, Herman could find no work. Yente urged him to
learn German, and although she herself did not speak it too
well, she had learned to read and understand it perfectly.

She could read the Bible with Herman Berg. Max would
give him lessons right in Yente's little home, and not only
did he learn the German language, but he learned God's
language, and God's plan for him. Soon the day came when
he accepted Christ as his Messiah and Lord.

It was around the end of July when Yente could scarcely
do any outside work, as she was expecting early in August,
that Herman told her of his decision for Christ. In the meantime he had visited Benjamin at the sanatorium on several
occasions, and there too he had had earnest conversations
regarding the Messiah of Israel. Yente's testimony and Benjamin's complete faith had puzzled him at first. But he soon
realized that it could only be the power of a living God sustaining them through all their trials, and he too longed for
that assurance and peace. On accepting the Lord, Herman
too experienced that new surge of life and hope which is
given to every believer.

Soon after he found odd jobs to do and he did them well.

He repaired bicycles and sewing machines, saving every "pfennig" for the fare which he needed to send his wife and children who were eagerly waiting to join him. Yente helped him in every way possible, sharing her last crust of bread with him.

## Lydia

But soon the time arrived when it was Mr. Berg's turn to be a help too. It was when a little girl, Yente's fifth child, arrived. It was then that he would come and look after the children.

David had heard of Yente's condition and came the day after the baby was born, bringing with him gifts of food and clothing for all.

Yente pondered over what they should name the new baby. She opened her Bible at Acts 16 and her eyes fell upon verses 14 and 15—

"And a certain woman named Lydia, a seller of purple, of the city of Thyatira, which worshipped God, heard us: whose heart the Lord opened, that she attended unto the things which were spoken of Paul.

"And when she was baptized, and her household, she besought us, saying, if ye have judged me to be faithful to the Lord, come into my house, and abide there. And she constrained us."

Ah, Lydia, she thought. That's a beautiful name. I will call my child Lydia, and may she be faithful to the Lord, and as willing to love and serve His brethren even as her namesake.

And Lydia it was.

## Chapter Nine

# The Steep and Winding Path

YENTE's stamina was remarkable. On the third day after the birth of Lydia she was up and about, singing and cooking and washing and cleaning, so much so, that her German neighbors who could scarcely believe their ears, came in to see this unusual woman, who cared so little for herself but so much for the things of God.

She seemed never to tire of "preaching" to them, and yet they could not resent her, for although handicapped by her husband's sickness and with insufficient food for her little ones, to say nothing of herself, she always smiled and went about with a song on her lips and in her heart. Her neighbors marvelled. "How could a woman recuperate so quickly", they asked one another. "Why it took most of us about two weeks to recover after our children were born. She must have the strength of a Russian Cossack", they concluded. Yet they could not help admiring her. Some of them even offered to help take care of her children now and then. Poverty was nothing new in the neighborhood where Yente lived. In fact nobody could boast of an abundance of this world's goods, yet none was so devoid of basic necessities as was Yente. "Diese Juedin ist brav" (This Jewish woman has courage), they all agreed.

## Benjamin Recovers

At last after long waiting and hoping Benjamin was well enough to leave the sanatorium. A family conclave was held in which David Fogel, Preacher Sommer, and the newly-found friend in need, Herman Berg, took part. It was felt that the best thing for Benjamin and Yente would be to move back to Kassel where many Christian friends would be glad to welcome them. Herman also decided to cast in his lot with the Sitenhofs.

And so early in 1909 the "trek back" began. Wistfully Yente sighed and wondered, "Shall I ever find a place I can really call home?"

She was only 26 but already a mother of five children, and her life thus far had been a constant wandering and pilgrimage to parts unknown and uncharted. Out of a longing heart came a song which she had recently heard in the Bruder Gemeinschaft (Brethren Fellowship):

"Wo findet die Seele die Heimat der Ruh!"

(Where shall the soul find the haven of rest)

But out of the depths of her being the answer came:

"Yente you have been a pilgrim all your life, but in all your wanderings did not your God lead you step by step and walk with you all the steep path?"

And Yente was satisfied that God was leading and she must follow.

Benjamin though still wan and delicate, was improving all the time, but the doctor advised him to go slow and not to spend himself by long hours of work. He was getting stronger day by day, and in due course he took up the burden of breadwinner again. His talents as a cabinet maker and builder stood him in good stead. His right hand did not forget her cunning during the period of enforced idleness.

## Another Reunion

In the meantime Herman Berg had saved enough money to bring his family over from Russia. And then the welcome day came when the little home which Yente had helped to prepare for the new arrivals, was ready to receive them. Yente had thought of everything, even of the vase of flowers on the table.

Herman was so anxious to tell his wife about the Messiah right after her arrival. He prayed fervently that she would not be too shocked upon learning of this.

It was a happy party which met the little family at the station, and soon they were home celebrating the joyful occasion with coffee and cake. At last Herman's prayer had been answered and his loved ones were with him in Germany. At the table he thanked God for this. Unused to such prayer, it so shocked his wife that she sat in ponderous silence for the rest of the evening, wondering what had come upon her husband. Herman however appeared unconcerned. "Oh that he might always be strong in the Lord", thought Yente and Benjamin.

In spite of his physical weakness Benjamin tried valiantly to keep his family provided with food and shelter. One of his lungs had been permanently sealed, and any strain taxed him. Yet he was able to follow his occupation, and with care and rest, which Yente encouraged him to take, his health gradually improved.

The three years 1909 to 1911 were happy years of family life and Christian fellowship; of physical growth for the children and spiritual maturity for their parents. All this time, however, Benjamin was burdened for the mission field, and especially for his own people the Jews. This thought was with him day and night. The desire to go into full-time service for the Lord gripped him to such an extent that he and Yente had regular prayer sessions, imploring the Lord that if it be His will He would make the way clear and send him.

## The Call to Argentina

It came to pass that one day several missionaries, natives of Kassel, came home on furlough. Benjamin confided his earnest desire to these men and asked their advice concerning South America. He was then told that there was an increasing Jewish population on this distant continent, especially in Argentina, and all of them were in great need of the Gospel. And who could better present it to them than a Hebrew Christian—one of their own flesh and blood?

To Benjamin this was a clear indication that Argentina was the land whither the Lord wanted him to go as His messenger. With this in view he took an intensive course of Bible study.

Then one day an invitation came to Benjamin from a group of Brethren in Argentina who were deeply concerned by the lack of a Christian testimony to Israel in their midst. They had heard about this young brother and wanted him to come over. But would he be willing to come alone at first and later on bring his family over?

At first the idea of going alone did not appeal to him. How could he leave Yente with five children, the youngest three years of age, even if only for a short while, to fend for themselves? No, he could not do that. And yet the more he thought of it the more convinced he became that it was the Lord's will for him, and that the Lord would provide for them in his absence.

Of course he would be going out on faith, and that meant being left without any income at all. The amazing thing was that Yente encouraged him to go. She had observed him closely and knew that if he missed this opportunity, it would make him very unhappy. Benjamin had plans of working part time at his well-paying trade in Buenos Aires, hoping to send for his family in a very short time.

But Yente had already made plans in her own mind to work herself and to provide for the children. It would give her Benjamin time to settle down, complete the course of Bible studies in South America, and to prepare a home for their little ones when they would join him.

## The Departure

It was a chilly November day when Benjamin departed for South America. Yente had been busy packing the little luggage which he took along. She went about her daily chores with a resolute expression on her face. Now and then she would tell the children in a subdued voice that daddy was about to leave on a long journey and that they should be especially good. The children played "house" until dusk, gathered around the old pieces of luggage, whispering to one another. Their faces were eager as they made their own plans for their journey across the big ocean. Didn't mother tell them that in a very  short time they too would follow their daddy?

Upstairs in the big bedroom Yente opened every drawer and every closet to see whether she had not forgotten something which might be useful for Benjamin on the long journey. There was the warm scarf which David had sent him for Christmas and which she had kept aside. She drew it out of its hiding place and looked at it lovingly with tears streaming down her cheeks.

Yes, she must show a brave face to the children. She must not let them know how her heart ached. She was determined that Benjamin should go on alone, and if it was God's will, she would follow with the children. But deep down in her heart she had a sense of foreboding. Benjamin was not strong. He had never been the same since his sanatorium days. His cough had not left him entirely and she was afraid of the hot climate in the Argentine. How would it affect his health?

Somehow she could not help feeling that she would not see Benjamin for a long, long time. Yes, she knew that she would have to be the breadwinner for her little brood of five, and always she thought of the attitude of the German people and how, in spite of everything, she was a foreigner in a foreign land. Her many Christian friends, who loved her as their own, stood by her and had promised Benjamin to take care of her. But she knew that feeling of loneliness even in the Christian circles when careless words and looks seemed to say, "What are you, a Jewess, doing here among us good German Christians?" Even the faith which should have bound them together and made them one, did not always seem to overcome the long ingrained inhibitions and deeprooted distrust.

She went downstairs with a heavy heart, busied herself about the kitchen, prepared supper, washed the children one by one—as was her usual methodical practice—and brushed the girls' hair, all the while not saying a word. But the tenseness of her expression revealed what was in her innermost thoughts. There she was, barely twenty-nine years of age, alone in a strange country with five little ones looking into her eyes for bread and comfort. But the Lord would strengthen her she knew. Her prayers would go up morning and night. She had complete faith. Had she not experienced His wonderful power all these years since her conversion?

The table laid, the children sat down quietly in an atmosphere of expectancy. They ate their food looking at one another with their large, sad eyes, wondering what was going to happen next. Toward the end of the meal there was a sound of footsteps on the path outside. The front door was hastily opened and Benjamin came in. As he entered the room he whispered something to Yente, and as if they had rehearsed their part, both made ready to say goodbye. The kerosene lamp on the table shed an uncanny glow, emphasizing the shadows in the far corners of the room. Nothing seemed to have changed, and yet to Yente everything had changed. It was as if she was set adrift in a boat in midocean without a compass. Whither now? There was no time to be lost. Benjamin had just whispered to her that he did not wish her to accompany him.

With an expression of utter sadness on his face, Benjamin walked up to each in turn, gave a hurried kiss, embraced Yente for one brief moment, took his black hat, picked up his small bags, and was gone. The children sat in their places motionless. Yente came and took her place beside them, and as if by mutual silent agreement, each buried their head in their hands. The owl in the arbor outside called its night cry—as usual. Or was there an added tone of haunting sadness this evening? Could it be true that they were left alone?

## Chapter Ten

# A Hard School

LEFT alone with a family of five growing children, Yente made her plans to keep the wolf from the door. She was determined that while there was breath in her and the good Lord above, her children should not suffer want. She would carry on until the day when they would be able to join Benjamin in Argentina.

Frau Emma Schmidt, the farmer's wife, had promised her the early morning delivery of butter, eggs and apples to sell. Before dawn every morning she would hurry to the station at four o'clock to collect the produce that she might be first on the market. Then, when she had sold out, she could run home to get the children their breakfast and by eight o'clock have the children off to school and kindergarten. Then she could hurry along to Mr. K. to do the chores in his home and be back by two o'clock in time to collect the large lamb's wool sacks. She mended a stack every week. After three hours work at the sacks, she could cook a good meal for the children, deliver her sacks after supper, get the children to bed, and then do her own housework.

Then there was also Frau H. who had asked her to come to do her washing if she could spare the time. On top of all this if need be there was the Insurance Company which asked her to clean their offices from three to four at night.

Elizabeth, her eldest child, was eleven and a great help to her mother with the children. She would bring them home from school and take care of them like a real little mother. Elizabeth was dependable. Really a good child—

bless her. Her heart was flooded with warmth thinking of her and her little flock—"the poor little pigeons."

Her thoughts were interrupted by little Lydia who was rubbing her eyes and crying that she wanted to go to bed. Elizabeth came round to her mother's chair, and stroking her hair, whispered that she would put the children to bed and let mother rest. The two boys demurred a little, but after their elder sister gave them a stern look, they scampered off to bed.

Meantime word went around among friends that Benjamin Sitenhof had left for the mission field. The news was a surprise. They would have liked to have given him a real sendoff. But Yente explained that he had managed to secure passage at the last moment, and had hurried his departure not knowing when another opportunity might be available. Only a small group of friends came to a special prayer meeting conducted by Pastor Sommer, committing Benjamin to God for his distant voyage and future work.

### The Cottage with the Red Roof and "Laube"

By the time Yente got word from Benjamin that he had arrived safely in Buenos Aires, she had so organized her life that her children lacked for nothing. They lived in one of the red-roofed little cottages, forming a crescent around an open courtyard, with a little green yard in the center, the "green pastures" of all residents, especially their children and their dogs. Their cottage was the last one and ended at a high wall dividing the next street.

Outside the little home was an arbor with a roof fixed to the high wall and overgrown with ivy. They called it the "Laube" in German. It was Yente's favorite spot. There she would gather the five children whenever she had a moment to spare and tell them Bible stories and make plans for the time when they would join daddy. The "Laube" was the pride and joy of the family. There Elizabeth, the eldest, would play house with the younger children. The "Laube" was the children's own "house" in a special way and many were the happy hours spent there.

### All This and Cake Too

The boys, Ernest 9 and Jacob 7, would delight in climbing up the sides of the trellis to see who could reach the top first, and screams of delight would be heard from the winner. Here the children would invariably gather around mother when she came home from her day's work with the "surprise." For Yente always managed somehow to procure a surprise for her brood, be it ever so small. Sometimes it was only a small bar of chocolate or a broken crumb cake bought at the baker at a much reduced price. Sometimes it was hard candy. But always there was something to make their hearts glad.

The crumb cake or broken doughnuts or simply cake crumbs were most popular with the children. Moved by sympathy for the hardworking mother and her children, a young woman at the bakery shop saved all the "broken cakes and cookies," filled a bag, and as Yente would pass the shop at night, beckon to her and let her have it for 10 pfenning. Sometimes it would be a very large bag. Yente had a suspicion that this kind soul who knew her circumstances, would break up the cakes on purpose so that she could let her have them at 10 pfenning. So Yente's children had cake too.

"People are very kind to us" Yente said to herself. Though she worked hard, she felt that strength was flowing into her being from a secret well of energy. Her little home was spotless, her children clean, nourished, and their clothing mended. She was a Jewess watched with scrutinizing eyes by everybody. And so she felt it was up to her not to invite any unfavorable comments, especially among the painstakingly clean German housewives. She was obsessed with a fear that if she would lower her standards of cleanliness she might be referred to as "Die Schmutzige Juedin."

The older children would go to school and the three younger ones to kindergarten, thus giving Yente most of the day to do outside work. She went from one job to the other keeping strictly to schedule every day, and by the time she reached home, cooked a meal, and Elizabeth helped her get the children to bed, she felt weary.

The spring and summer months seemed so much easier, for then she had fruit to sell at the market and did less housecleaning for other people. How exacting were the German people. But she came up to their neat standards. She even found time to make her children's clothing, including the boys' sailor suits. The neighbors marvelled at her when on Sunday morning the Sitenhof children would appear all fresh and clean with starched and ironed dresses on the girls, and spick and span suits on the boys.

But winter proved a great strain on Yente. Washing by hand large family washes in damp cellars, and rinsing them in three or four changes of icy cold water, told on her in time. Her skirts would freeze and look like a hoop by the time she got home. She would have to "defrost" them in the warm kitchen, to the delight of the children, but to the damaging of her health. Gradually she developed rheumatism and had to give up the big washes. Instead she took on a job cleaning law offices, which necessitated her getting up at 4 o'clock in the morning, and waxing and polishing on her knees for two hours or more.

## A Pilgrim in a Foreign Land

Meantime in Argentina Benjamin was trying to get established. The group of Christians in Buenos Aires welcomed him warmly, rejoicing that at last their prayers were answered and a messenger was sent to bear a Christian witness to the ever growing Jewish community. Benjamin gave himself wholeheartedly to his work. There were so many poor and wretched people in that great metropolis of South America, a city of vice and degradation. His heart ached for these souls adrift. Some of them were carried away from their homes by cunning and deceit.

To many disillusioned and heartbroken souls Benjamin was not only a link with their old homes in Europe but a harbinger of hope. In his spare time Benjamin worked at completing a course of Bible study, qualifying him for full time service in the Gospel.

Friends rallied around so that now and then he was even able to send some money to his family. This, however, seldom reached Yente, as the mails were pilfered frequently in those days. But Yente wrote him encouraging letters, telling him only of the bright events in their lives and keeping to herself the burdens she carried and the sacrifices she had to endure to keep a roof over the heads of the five little ones, and the wolf from the door. She told him how she was being encouraged by the brethren, especially Prediger Sommer, and how they looked forward to a reunion soon. Why they even discussed at the prayer meeting the question of sending Yente and her children over to Benjamin, that the family might be together.

But as the funds for the fares for six could not be raised,

the months and two years went by in an endless struggle for Yente.

In the meantime Benjamin wrote that the hot and humid climate was exacting a heavy toll on his frail health. He even had to be hospitalized for a few months in 1913 and it seemed that it would be wise for him to return to Germany. But he too had no money for the journey, so he decided to work and save for his fare.

## In a Princely Home

It was in the spring of 1913 that Yente made the acquaintance of a servant of God, who came to her help in a marvelous way. The law offices where she worked had changed their cleaning schedule. Much to Yente's relief she was able to do her work from three to five in the afternoons. One day Yente came a little early to her work and on entering the offices noticed at a table a tall military looking man in conference with one of the attorneys.

This attorney had taken a human interest in Yente and had questioned her on several occasions about herself and her circumstances. He had told her he thought she looked too refined to be doing such hard work, and sometimes wondered whether it was not too much for her. She had told him all about herself and Benjamin, and he had promised to help her find less exhausting work.

Now he called her in and introduced her to his client, Major Von S., aide to the princely House of Hesse. He explained that there was a vacancy for a chambermaid at the Princess' residence, at which they resided only during the winter months, and he had recommended her for the work which was easy and well paid. Yente could scarcely believe her ears. Could it be that she a foreigner, could even as much as enter the household of the Princess? Yente was modest, and in her humble way she gave voice to her thoughts. "Say little and work well," the Major advised her, and you have the work. Thanking her would-be employer with tears in her eyes she ran home as on air. Gathering her five children about her she thanked her Heavenly Father who cared for them even more than she knew or expected.

Her hours were to be from 9:30 o'clock to three. After a special week of instruction by the housekeeper, she would be assigned to taking care of the rooms of the young princes, who were undergoing strict military training at the time under the supervision of the Major.

The next morning she was to present herself at the Major's office, and this interview she never forgot. He shook hands with her as she entered the office, saying, "Schwester (Sister) Sitenhof, I am a Christian and I know you are also, and I am your friend." So this, thought Yente, was God's messenger to her, even as an angel in disguise.

He seemed to know every detail about her, even to the date of her conversion. They had prayer together before he explained to her the duties she would be expected to perform. The dignity and importance of this man's position was evident to her. His quiet, calm and yet authoritative way of speaking was mingled with kindness and understanding. He was about "sixty years young," white-haired, broad-shouldered, and had a military bearing. He cut an impressive figure.

"My child," he said, "if ever you are in difficulty, come to me, and I will try and help you. Do not let the servants engage you in conversation, and apart from courtesy, do not mingle with them. There will be opposition," he said. "Some may be against you, but let it not worry you, I will stand behind you." With these reassuring words he dismissed her, and as if in a dream Yente commenced her duties.

The housekeeper, a large heavyset woman with Prussian background, frowned openly when she first met Yente. In the first place, because she looked too frail and inexperienced, and secondly, because she suspected a "foreigner" in her. But because the Major, who was the respected "head" of the household, had recommended her so highly, she was silent. But Yente learned well and applied herself to her work so that before the week was over, the housekeeper knew she had a reliable worker in her. Above all, the unobtrusive way in which she went about her work, without taking time out with the others to gossip whenever there was a chance, broke down all opposition to her appointment. She had no fault to find with Yente.

What a relief for Yente to have a regular and dignified position like this, enabling her to discontinue some of the tortuous jobs she had bravely been doing for more than two years. She did continue her early morning country produce selling, for that enabled her to feed her five darlings butter, eggs and apples. With her new work in the Royal household she was able to eke out a little more than a mere existence.

At weekends she would take the children on their weekly treat, a picnic on the "Brusselsberg," a suburban beauty spot where one could sit under a large tree. They could eat their own food at a picnic table and order without embarrassment five glasses of hot chocolate for the children and "Kaffee mit Schlagsahne" (coffee with whipped cream) for herself. All week she and the children would look forward to the picnic and when they reached the top of the hill she would be one of them, playing their games, romping in the grass, hiding behind trees, and feeding the squirrels.

At such times she looked so young and carefree that other picnickers would think she was the nursemaid, until to their astonishment they heard the children call her "Mama."

Yente's faith in the Lord waxed stronger day by day. At the end of a perfect day when the sun was setting, she loved to gather her five children around her and before returning home, they would lift their hearts to God and sing hymns they knew so well. Sometimes strangers would gather around the little group and join in. When the folks who came there to picnic discovered that Yente's husband was a missionary in South America, their interest grew. They wanted to know more about this unusual family whose joy in the Lord, from the oldest girl down to the baby, shone in their faces.

## "Old Soldiers Never Die"

On the third floor of their little house in a garret room there lived an old pensioner, "der alte Herr Riehm." His maiden sister kept house for him. He was 81 and old Mr. Riehm looked the typical Santa Claus of picture post-cards, with his long flowing white beard, twinkling, deepset blue eyes, and sparkling sense of humor. He was a veteran of the Franco-German War of 1870. The children just loved him, a love reciprocated with mischievous affection. They would tease each other mercilessly, but the day always ended with the children gathered around the fire at old Papa Riehm's feet, listening to his exciting and inexhaustible war experiences, to which he added every time, drawing upon an unfailing memory and lively imagination.

He would smoke a yard long curly pipe. The children loved to watch his venerable wrinkled old face through the smoke screen. Often Yente was able to do a little extra work at night and leave the children happy in the care of old father Riehm. He had nobody in the world besides his sister, and so he claimed and enjoyed as his own the five little soldiers who looked up at him as the hero who won the Franco-German war almost singlehanded.

He never failed to remember each child's birthday with a little gift. It was his custom to tie the gift on the end of a string and dangle it out of his window until the "birthday child" would throw open the window below and claim it by pulling it in amidst the laughter and excitement of the rest.

But old Herr Riehm was an unbeliever and Yente pleaded with him whenever she had the opportunity, to put his trust in Jesus. At first he scoffed good naturedly and took little notice of what she said. But when he realized the strength of her faith and the part it played in her life, he became interested. One evening toward the end of 1913 Yente stopped him on his way out for his evening stroll, and asked him to make a decision for Christ there and then; to ask the Lord to forgive his sins and prepare him for eternal life. "Before it is too late," Yente told him, "accept Christ as your Saviour, and you will experience that peace which passes all understanding." He broke down and accepted the Lord. "If He means that much to you," he said, "then I will give Him a chance to mean that much to me. Your life has been a testimony to me of what God can do for a child of His. I too accept Him as my Saviour."

With those words the old man left the house. That very night on his way back to his upper room he missed his footing and fell backward down the two flights of stairs. Papa Riehm died instantly. Yente's little household was grief stricken, but in her heart there was a song for she knew that the old man died a believer and that his Captain was waiting to welcome the old warrior Home.

# Chapter Eleven

# The Powder Keg

WITH the coming of the Spring of the year 1914, tension in Europe was mounting daily. Long dormant national antagonisms smoldering throughout Europe for the last fifty years or more had accumulated enough explosive passions to blow up the continent and bring about a holocaust such as the world had not seen up to that day.

There was Germany feeling her oats after defeating France in 1870, and imposing the humiliating peace upon that republic. Her industries were growing but markets were dominated chiefly by powerful "John Bull" ruling the waves. There was France, still smarting from the humiliation and defeat inflicted upon her by Prussia, and waiting for the day to square ancient accounts with her Eastern neighbor. And in the East the Empire of the despotic czars, who felt that they were called to unite under the aegis of "Little Mother Russia" all the Slav nations of Europe.

Then there was the Austro-Hungarian Empire under Franz Joseph II, made up of a vast conglomeration of Slav and Balkan nations, built around the backbone and strong arm of the German and Hungarian national element; a hodgepodge of nationalities, seething, striving and wrestling for independence—jealous and suspicious of each other, smarting under ancient wrongs. A veritable powder keg.

The match to this powder keg was the assassination on June 28th of Archduke Ferdinand, Crown Prince to the throne of the Hapsburgs of Austria. He was murdered by a fanatical student while visiting the city of Sarajevo in the little Kingdom of Serbia, cocky because of her alliance with big brother Russia.

## The Beating of the Drums

In Germany more than elsewhere there was the certainty of impending war. Everybody was asking not whether, but how soon would war come.

The public places and show windows of elegant stores in Kassel were decorated with colored reproductions of Kaiser Wilhelm II, resplendent in his uniform of a Field-marshal of the army, and having as his headgear the pickelhaube, the sharp-pointed tall helmet of a German military commander. His steely eyes, his upward pointed and well-waxed mustache, his chest covered with decorations and shining medals, bespoke of confidence and even defiance.

The Kaiser's picture was kept company by that of the stern and imposing faces of his field-marshals and generals, Von Moltke, Von Ludendorf, Von Hindenburg, and others.

The passing public looked admiringly and with pride at them. Even when their lips were silent, their eyes seemed to say plainly, "Surely with these great men leading us we cannot possibly lose."

The strains of "Deutschland, Deutschland, Ueber Alles" came from beer halls, patriotic meetings, and military bands leading marching men. Through the streets of the old garrison city of Kassel, one could hear the steady tramp, tramp, tramp, of hobnailed boots, soldiers marching in tact with the precision of a well-oiled and well-drilled machine.

The atmosphere was charged with confident and pugnacious patriotism. Foreigners and strangers were automatically suspect. "What were they doing in the Fatherland?" "Surely they must be spies."

### Suspected, Unwanted

Yente could feel the sidelooks of the people at her and her little family. Even at work some of her fellow-servants were looking askance at her and asking among themselves, "What is this Russian Jewess doing here? Is she a spy too? Why doesn't she pack up and go to Russia with her family where they belong anyway?" Yente continued her daily work as conscientiously as ever, still able to muster her smile. Calm on the surface, there was turmoil in her heart.

What was she to do, she asked herself, if war should come? Alone in an enemy country, with five little children and without means? Where could she go?

Benjamin's last letter from Buenos Aires, dated May 25, 1914, was rather vague about his return, although he did mention that he might take a boat to Europe any time during the summer. But on July 20th upon her return to the little house in Kassel, she found a telegram from England waiting for her. Benjamin had arrived in London sick and could not continue his journey. A letter was on the way.

A fierce midsummer storm with thunder and lightning

was gathering over her head. Would she be caught in the hurricane unsheltered and unprotected? Would she and her loved ones be swept away like helpless leaves torn from a tree? "Oh God," she prayed fervently and feverishly, "show me a way out and open a door of escape."

## "Go!"

On her way to work she ran into her good friend, the Major, who greeted her very friendly. He could see in her face that Yente was deeply perturbed. Her usual serene face and smiling eyes were now filled with hardly restrained tears.

He was a friend, of that she was certain. He would do everything to help her. The Major invited her to his office to discuss her position. He advised her that she must leave the country immediately even if it meant separation from her children for a time.

Yente's mind was in a whirl. What was this disaster that had come upon her so suddenly? Is this what she had slaved for all these years, hovering like a mother bird over her nest, trying to protect her chicks from harm and hurt? Was she now to be separated from her children, without knowing when they would be together again? To leave her little ones in a hostile country at the mercy of strangers?

Yes, the Major did mention Christian friends. But who would take care of five children? So they would each have to be in a different home. Her poor little lambs! How could she do it? And what a decision to have to make!

That day Yente went about her chores in a mechanical way, her mind hardly knowing what her hands were doing. Yet an intelligence greater than hers guided her hands at their accustomed duties.

In the evening after feeding her family and putting them to bed she fell upon her knees, and poured out her heart before her Lord, asking Him to lift the burden so suddenly thrust upon her shoulders. Would He undertake for her and the children, and whatever His will might be, would He make it clear to her! She got up from her knees strengthened.

And then the door bell rang. As she opened the door, there was Sister Paula, a Christian nurse whom she had known among the chapel people. She came to say goodby to Yente and her little friends. She whispered in confidence to Yente that she had received her mobilization papers from the army and was to leave next morning. So that was it, thought Yente. War was sure to come any moment. Sister Paula begged her not to mention to anyone about her mobilization papers as it was still a secret. But she wanted to warn Yente. And she was anxious to say goodby to all of them, especially her little favorite, Lydia. She walked into the bedroom where the five year old Lydia was sleeping peacefully. She stroked her dark curly hair and crept on tiptoe downstairs.

Within the next three months Sister Paula gave her life as a nurse in the front lines in East Prussia.

## Benjamin's Return to London

At last Benjamin's letter arrived. He was laid up in a room in London, he wrote, with a high temperature and a racking cough. The doctor had warned him not to be moved. Kind friends from a London missionary society were attending to his need. But to journey in his condition was out of the question.

He was conscious of the danger to Yente and the children in Germany if war should break out, and he begged her to come on, even should it be necessary without the children, so that they could both work together from the outside to get the children over. Leave everything, he said in his letter and come quickly.

When she finished reading, Yente thought, how strange that her husband and the Major unaware of each other, should have the same plan for her. This then must be the Lord's will. In spite of the heartache and uncertainty this would bring into her life, she had to go through with the plan. Oh, how could she be torn from her young children, especially little Lydia, barely six years old!

Of course Herr Sommer offered to have his godchild, little Marie, in his own home. He wished he could take all the children, but Mrs. Sommer and he were now advanced in years and they would hardly be able to do that, and do justice to the children. Then and there he telephoned to several Christian friends inviting them to come that evening to his home to talk things over.

At the Major's advice Yente did not continue her chores at the Princess' household. He told her to wind up all her affairs within the next few days and the time of her departure would be as soon as her exit permit came through. Yente got busy.

The three large wicker hampers stored in the cellar were brought up and all her worldly possessions accumulated through the years of her wanderings were packed in them. These too were the promise of a new home—somewhere—sometime—God willing. The precious down and feather beds which her father-in-law, Abraham Sitenhof of blessed memory, had given her before she left Warsaw some years ago, were placed at the very bottom. They could absorb a lot of shock. The little bits of china and crockery were packed in between, and a few of the more precious little possessions which a family acquires as it journeys along life's winding path—"Rachel's domestic gods"—which she found it so difficult to abandon forever. Poor, pitiful Yente, pack yourself up again and go on! Whither?

Last time when she packed to go from Warsaw to Germany when she decided to bring her Benjamin back from Jesus to the faith of his fathers, she at least knew exactly where she was going. This time, not even that was granted to her. Where would she unpack her meager belongings again? Where would her home be?

In the evening she went back to Mr. Sommer's home. The friends had gathered and several had expressed willingness to take the children to their homes. There was the fine old Mrs. Lembke, the dentist's mother—she would be glad to have Elizabeth. She was already a big girl of 13 years and could certainly make herself useful after school. Her son the dentist would not mind taking Ernest. He lived in the suburbs and had a boy the same age and the two could be company for each other.

Mrs. Berg, the wife of Henry, whom she had led to Christ, offered to take Jacob, if nobody else would have him. She would gladly have received him in any case, but she had her own five little ones in cramped quarters. But if nothing more suitable could be found he would be welcome any way. What her children had, he would have also. "Whether you have seven or eight mouths to feed does not make much difference, so don't cry Yente", she argued, scolding her lovingly.

But what about little Lydia? Oh, if she could take Lydia with her! But no, that was not to be. The Major had warned her to leave all the children behind. Otherwise the arrangements might be imperiled.

## War

The assassination of Crown Prince Ferdinand of Austria brought a chain reaction series of explosions all over Europe. Exactly one month after that fateful event, Austria declared war on Serbia; Russia the ally of Serbia declared war on Austria; by August 1st Germany allied with Austria, declared war on Russia; and England and France allied with Russia, declared themselves on the side of the Czars.

Ernest, a serious youngster with sad eyes, was 11 years old. Anxious to help his mother, he decided to be a news boy. The first day of his new job he came home with a few unsold newspapers with screaming headlines "Germany at War."

Yente received the news calmly. Inside she knew that her faith was about to be tested to the utmost.

### Little Lydia

Now Yente was ready for the dread separation and journey. The only thing that remained to be taken care of was to find a home for little Lydia. She had made some effort to find a home with Christian friends, but so far not quite successfully. Friends were afraid a little girl might be too much wrapped up in her mother and become homesick.

Little Lydia could sense her beloved mommie's uneasiness. Mother did not tell her anything, but what are words to souls in love when every fleeting thought or passing shadow on the beloved face is a book written in more expressive idiom than any printed word could possibly be. And Lydia kept looking into mommie's beautiful eyes as if she were some unearthly creature or angel. How she loved to be with her—just to feel her presence! Conversation was hardly necessary. Her soulful dreamy eyes did all the talking.

How she loved in the evening to take off mother's shoes and bring her the old slippers. That was her little service and peculiar tribute to the one she loved. If only she could give mommie something that would tell of her great love. She was a little girl in love, and felt love's almost painful necessity to give its all, its very life, and all the most precious gifts it can dream of. But what could she, a little girl give? "One day when she grows up she will buy mommie the most beautiful slippers in all the world, red ones as soft and caressing as her love."

Finally a long awaited message arrived from the Reverend

Friedrich Wolfgang Lembke, Pastor of the Lutheran Church some 80 miles away. He was a brother of the dentist who agreed to take Elizabeth. In his letter the pastor said that since they had no children of their own they would be glad to take care of little Lydia. He would come the next day to take her with him.

Now all was settled. The children were taken care of and Yente was free to take her journey the very next day.

That evening it seemed that all the friends she had in Kassel gathered around her to do something for Yente and her children. There were Mr. and Mrs. Herman Berg with a hot meal for the family so that Yente would not have to do any cooking in the midst of packing. Herr Prediger and Mrs. Sommer came in to say goodby and to speak to the several friends who promised to take care of the children.

After a season of prayer with the friends they all bid her goodby and Godspeed. Some embraced her fondly and wished her speedy reunion with all her loved ones. Then they departed. Yente was left alone with her children and with her God.

She put the children to bed with exceptional affection and tenderness. None of them knew as yet that mother was to leave. Why should she rob her darlings of one night's sleep before her departure? The morning will bring sorrow and heartache enough. Only Elizabeth, the eldest, had been taken into full confidence. Yente looked with longing and infinite sadness at each child, reposed in sleep and blissful unawareness.

She stayed up the rest of the night, thinking her aching thoughts and praying imperceptibly in her heart. The Lord was her Shepherd and the Shepherd of her little lambs. Surely He would guide them to green pastures and still waters.

The last bit of packing was completed. Tomorrow Yente would pick up the papers at the Major's house and go straight to the station. Tomorrow would be August 12th and also Lydia's sixth birthday. She felt a strong urge to cry—but no, she must not give way to weakness—later in the train perhaps—now she must be strong.

## Chapter Twelve
# Rachel Weeping for Her Children

NEXT morning there was a hushed silence at the breakfast table. Yente recalled in her mind that day three years ago when Benjamin was departing for South America. There was the same tugging at the heart as when you part from loved ones, the same feeling of sorrow and yearning for dear ones still with you, and yet already missed.

The children, all dressed in their Sunday best, questioned Yente as to where they were going. They knew they were leaving the house, but how could Yente tell them the truth? If she would begin to tell the arrangements made for them, how they would be scattered like leaves shaken from a tree by strong winds, she would break down. She would be in no position to travel. She would have to abandon all her carefully arranged plans. It was too much for her. It would be more than the children could bear.

She must harden her heart and do violence to her feelings. One by one she put them off, seemingly hard and cold, saying, "You will find out soon enough."

After breakfast, Mr. Sommer's sister, known to the family as Aunt Bess, came to escort them all to the station. Little Lydia stood in the corner as was her wont, thumb in mouth, eyes wide, big and sad, looking with bewilderment on the proceedings and the hustle and bustle of the last moments.

What was going on here? Dread seized her little heart and squeezed till it hurt. She clung to her mother, eyes ablaze with unspoken and unanswered questions.

At last they were ready to go to the station. Each child carried a little bundle of belongings, little Lydia dragging along her beloved doll mommie made for her out of small scraps. Each child was spick and span, with shoes highly polished. The girls' dresses were starched beautifully, their

hair brushed and combed. Their short pigtails looked as
if they too were starched. Each face was a study of bewildered emotions. Youthful eagerness and anticipation of
the unknown, mingled with fear and anxious forebodings.

The farewell was quick, the children scarcely realizing
what was happening.

Yente had told Elizabeth and Aunt Bess to take Lydia
away as quickly as possible. They crossed the big square
to the station, Aunt Bess telling the children that mother
was going to get the tickets. In a flash Yente was gone,
without as much as a kiss for little Lydia.

The child looked back with that same puzzled expression
of bewilderment on her face, hesitating for a moment to go
on. As if from nowhere Pastor Lembke and his wife joined
them. He immediately diverted her attention to the small
doll which she was holding, commenting on what a fine doll
it was. Lydia grasped it eagerly as if for comfort. "Come
with me little girl," he encouraged her. "I have many beautiful dolls in my home and you may play with them."

One by one the children left the little group. Elizabeth
was taking brother Jack to the small village outside Kassel
where he was going to stay with a relative of Mr. Sommer's.
Ernest was asked to follow Mr. Schneider. Quickly they entered a waiting cab and drove away. Aunt Bess embraced
Marie and hurried away.

## A Child's World Breaks Like a Bubble

Lydia, the youngest of them all felt that strange things
were taking place in her small world. Somehow everything
seemed to be melting away before her eyes and her little
mind was a turmoil of confusion. They were now crossing
again the station square, back to the city, but her eyes had
not left the spot where her mother had disappeared. She
felt someone was holding her hand, but she dared not turn
her head to look, fearing she might lose the spot where
mother disappeared. And then all in a rush reality broke
upon her, like the angry billows of a stormy sea.

A man and a woman, each holding one of her hands, were
taking her away quickly, away from her darling mother,
away from life and its very essence—mother. She was
blinded by hot tears streaming down her strained little face.
Who were these strangers? She had never seen them before.

## Marching as to War

In the meantime Yente entered the railway carriage. Now a flood of grief and heartache overwhelmed her. She broke down completely and sat sobbing until the train left the station. There was nothing she could do now but leave her children in the hands of God and pray for a speedy reunion.

With the clairvoyance and intuition given to those filled with a great love, which sometimes borders almost on the supernatural, she could see clearly the terrible experiences waiting for her "orphans," at the mercy of strangers in an alien land—at war.

The rest of the train was filled with soldiers going to the front. The cars were decorated with national flags and boastful inscriptions. "Nach Paris!" (To Paris!), or "Siegreich wollen wir Frankreich schlagen!" (Victoriously we shall defeat France!) At every station the wives and children, sweethearts and friends gathered to see their men folk off. There was much waving of flags and outbursts of patriotic songs. "Die Wacht am Rhein" (The Watch on the Rhine), "Deutschland, Deutschland Ueber Alles" (Germany, Germany above All), and military marches which had become so familiar the last few weeks, were sung heartily to the accompaniment of local brass bands.

In spite of all that was going on around her, Yente felt completely alone. She sat in the corner of her compartment glancing at the jubilation which greeted the train at each station, as new soldiers boarded the train and said farewell to friends and relatives. There was much laughing and suppressed crying of mothers, wives, and sweethearts. It seemed that they would never stop coming, these soldiers with their knapsacks and their families. More cars were added to the train as it went on its way, more soldiers, more military equipment.

As they travelled westward they would pass trains going in the opposite direction toward the East. Only these trains were marked with different inscriptions, like, "Schnellzug nach Moskau!" (Express to Moskow!), or "Russland Kaput!" (Russia is done for!). They too were filled with soldiers, some young recruits with the fuzz of youth on their chins, and some bearded reservists, all dressed in the gray uniforms of the Imperial and Royal German Infantry. The brass buckles of their belts inscribed with the words "Gott mit Uns." Their trousers were tucked in below the knees in the tops of their shining high boots.

Yente wondered how long she would be on the way. Normally the journey took two days, but in war time there was no telling. It might even take a week or more to reach neutral Holland.

The Major had given her an envelope that morning that she had not yet opened. She looked for it in her pocket and unsealed it. There she found her ticket to England via neutral Holland, and extra money in Dutch and English currency. How thoughtful of him! He had indeed proved a worthy friend.

By nightfall Yente was so exhausted that she sank back into her corner and tried to sleep. But the din of the military bands, now apparently travelling on the train, made it quite impossible. She was in such an exhausted state from the mental and physical strain, that she could not relax.

On arriving at the German-Dutch frontier, the train stopped for inspection. War breeds fear and suspicion. Every stranger is a potential enemy or even a spy. So custom and passport inspection dragged on endlessly for hours. Yente wondered whether she would ever reach London. The passport official looked at her with suspicion. When she produced her papers, he asked her numerous questions, and shook his head in bewilderment. What was this beautiful young woman with a tear-stained face doing on a military train?

Finally after more than two weeks of travel and being shunted to sidelines to allow the passage of trains with wounded soldiers, her train reached Hook of Holland on the English Channel. There she embarked on a small cross channel boat for Harwich.

All night she sat on deck, saturated with the fine spray of the sea and her own tears and shivering with cold. All night long she swayed with every motion of the boat, as well as her own body—torn with grief—a living statue of sorrowing motherhood. The words of Jeremiah came to her memory, words which she read only a few days ago:

"Thus saith the Lord: a voice was heard in Ramah, lamentation, and bitter weeping: Rachel weeping for her children refused to be comforted for her children, because they were not.

"Thus saith the Lord; Refrain thy voice from weeping, and thine eyes from tears; for thy work shall be rewarded, saith the Lord; and they shall come again from the land of the enemy.

"And there is hope in thine end, saith the Lord, that thy children shall come again to their own border."—Jeremiah 31:15-17.

"Oh, Mother Rachel," cried Yente, "I know your grief, for I too am a mother and my children are not. Oh, that the God who comforted you might also comfort my aching heart."

It seemed as if the gray mist of hoary time between her and her distant ancestress, Mother Rachel, had suddenly disappeared. She, Yente, weeping for her children; her own mother Rachel, the wife of Jakob the Russian soldier, Rachel who died trampled by the hoofs of the Cossack horses, Rachel who gave her life for her little ones, and that other Rachel the matriarch of the Hebrew race, had all become one.

It was a kinship of flesh and blood very real, and keenly felt. But it was more than that. It was the kinship of suffering womanhood, a kinship of all mothers through the ages, who since the days of Mother Eve have cried over their beloved Abels and wept for the crimes of their ungodly but no less beloved Cains.

At dawn the English shores near Harwich appeared on the near horizon, the sight of which stirred her mind with memories of her first visit to England some fifteen years ago. When she disembarked in Harwich there was the same suspicious scrutiny of the custom and immigration officials as on the German-Dutch border. Her Russian passport was in her favor, for the Empire of the Czars was the ally of England. But this woman coming from Germany already at war with England, was a puzzle just the same.

Finally, after checking and rechecking her credentials she was admitted to England and boarded the long train with little cars which was to take her to Liverpool Street Station in London. On the way, hungry and weary, she ordered her breakfast, a poached egg on toast, marmalade, and a large pot of strong tea. She felt better now and was confidently looking forward to meeting her husband in London.

## In London Again

But at Liverpool Street Station, Benjamin was not there. Instead two ladies who introduced themselves to her as Miss Taylor and Miss Fried greeted her cordially. They embraced her warmly and explained that Benjamin was home with a slight fever. He wanted to come to the station, but the mission doctor absolutely forbade him to do so. Again her heart felt heavy. A horse drawn hansom took them through the East End of London, where she found Benjamin in a small upstairs apartment waiting for her.

Looking at the wan face of her beloved, she was torn between joy and concern. Three years of absence is like an eternity when it means separation from a loved one—and he looked so thin and pale. Oh, she would soon mother him and coax him back to health!

They talked for hours, each full of questions and experiences which filled the years of absence from one another. But overshadowing the joy of reunion was the constant remembrance that their children were alone among strangers in Germany. They must find some way of bringing them over to England as soon as possible. They would leave no stone unturned. They would storm Heaven and earth to bring this about.

## Chapter Thirteen

# The Enchanted Village

THE train journey from Kassel to Roedeldorf where the Rev. Lembke was pastor seemed like a nightmare to six year old Lydia. She sat in deep silence, stunned and numbed from head to toe. Any moment she expected to wake up and hear the comforting voice of her dear mother. But mother was far away.

When they finally reached their destination and her escorts hustled her out of the train, Lydia woke up to the realization that she had been lured away into a strange place. Then the little girl began to fight for her freedom. In the train they had said very little to her, but now on the dusty country road they tried to explain that they were taking her to their home to live with them.

For the tired little girl all this was too much to comprehend. Like an outraged and trapped animal, the child fought, weeping, kicking, and even biting the hands which led her.

The Lembkes had no children of their own and did not seem to understand the emotions of this child. In vain did they try to calm her. To the child it seemed that they walked and partly dragged her along past mountains and farmsteads, over bridges and through wooded sections—a tedious journey. But finally they reached the village of Roedeldorf. Actually, the whole journey was only two miles from the railroad station, but measured by the imagination of a tired and bewildered child it seemed a long journey into captivity.

The village was like one pictured in fairy tales. In spite of herself Lydia had to stop her weeping and take in the quaintness of the hamlet. The baaing of the sheep crossing a narrow bridge greeted her ears. The sheep dog and the shepherd boy followed close at their heels. In the distance a tall church steeple towered over the horizon. Just then the bells started pealing out their sweet music. What was that? It sounded so familiar. Yes, it was an evening hymn her darling mother used to sing—"So nimm denn meine Haende and fuehre mich. . ." (Take Thou my hand and lead me.)

Hot tears filled her eyes. Mrs. Lembke sensing the pathos of the moment, took the child's hand and drew her to herself. At heart she was a kindly woman, only cowed by an overbearing husband. It was the first gesture of understanding and sympathy which Lydia had experienced since that morning.

By that time the sun was sinking in the west. Worn out by the emotional strain the little girl submitted to the woman at her side and walked quietly the rest of the way, always coming closer to the church in the village. In spite of her grief, she could not help feeling that she was walking in a fairy-land. At a glance she took in the many delightful details of the scene. Her first impressions of the quaint hamlet of Roedeldorf remained with her always, a memory of beauty and sadness.

The village main street was narrow and cobbled. On either side were picture-book little white cottages with steps leading up to the entrance door. Then came the narrow bridge with two handrails which the shepherd with a staff in his hand was just crossing. Under the bridge ran a clear cool stream from which came distinctly the croaking of frogs.

They passed a large sow and four little baby pigs which made Lydia, who had never seen a real pig, cling to the lady. How white the baby pigs were, they looked so clean and scrubbed. And how their little wee tails curled in an upward spiral!

Soon the church came into full view—a beautiful structure and so like the picture in her story book. Across the road from the church was the manse. They stopped and the man said, "Well, here we are at home."

## The Manse

It was a gray austere looking stone two-story house, much too "grand" to be called home. They entered and at once it seemed a coldness gripped the child. A great English bulldog came bouncing down the stairs straight to his master, and standing on his hind legs reached up to his shoulders. "This is Brutus," said Mrs. Lembke. "Don't be afraid of him because he loves children, and I know you are going to be friends." Lydia had never before lived in a home with a dog. This magnificent animal with the big blue tongue of the pedigreed dog and sleek brown coat, fascinated the child.

The maid, Lieschen, an apple-cheeked country girl, whom Lydia learned to love right away greeted them warmly, and immediately took charge of her.

She was led to a second floor bedroom which was to be her very own. A large imposing bed greeted her as she entered. The thought of sleeping all alone in such a big bed made her shudder. She had always been used to cuddling up to her big sister Elizabeth, and on occasions the three girls had shared a double bed. Something about the room chilled her.

"You can leave your door open, Liebchen (darling)," said Lieschen, "if you are not used to sleeping alone. My room is right above yours, and I will hear you if you call."

There was something reassuring about Lieschen as she took the child into her arms and pressed her to her ample bosom. Her sense of security so suddenly and rudely shaken, returned to her for a moment.

Lydia took in some of the details of the large hall out of which all the bedrooms opened. There was a black ebony stand containing many long smoking pipes. On the front of the stand was a selection of leather dog whips, some plaited and quite thick. She wondered why should one dog need so many whips. But soon she forgot about it. There were also in the hall two large black cedar chests and she wondered what was inside.

"That room," said Lieschen, pointing to a formidable black carved door, "is the study of the Pastor. You must never enter it unless you are invited, dear child," she said. Later on the sight of that door would send chills down her back.

Supper in the dining room was brief and sparse. The child seemed so wrapped up in her tearful thoughts that she hardly heard Pastor Lembke as he tried to explain that they wanted to be friends and kind to her. Her mother had gone to England, he said, to meet her father, but because of the war between Germany and England it was not likely that she would see her mother in the near future.

After supper, as if looking for some diversion for the child, they took her upstairs, undressed her (not without a struggle) and gave her a bath. It would have been embarrassing enough for the child if Mrs. Lembke had attended to her, but when the Pastor himself proceeded to give her a bath—saying how much he enjoyed children—Lydia was outraged.

"Who are these horrible people," she kept saying to herself, "and why do they persist in tormenting me instead of leaving me alone?" After the bath, slippers and a nightgown were provided, and the special treat which the Pastor had promised her all the evening materialized.

## The Doll Which Could Say "Mama"

They took her to the attic and showed her large boxes full of toys. There were dolls of all descriptions—baby dolls and dolls that could say "Mama." Large dolls, small dolls, and medium-sized dolls. There were other toys also for boys, but Lydia had no eyes for those. Only the doll that said "Mama" held her spellbound. "These toys," explained the Pastor, "are for our Christmas party at the church. Every child will receive a gift then, and if you are a good little girl," he added, "you will get one too."

At that the child stopped crying and felt somewhat consoled. She thought if she only had a doll that said "Mama" she would not feel so forsaken. The very word "Mama" somehow was comforting. Finally they put her to bed after Pastor Lembke prayed with her. She never forgot that prayer—at least not the voice of the Pastor who uttered it.

## Lord and Master of the Manse

Pastor Lembke was a typical Prussian, a pastor by profession only, but his heart had never been touched by the kindliness of the gentle Saviour, the friend of little children. He was a hard man indeed. In his domain he was lord and master. He made sure that all and sundry knew about it too. In the Lembke household his word was law. If his wife ever differed with him she never dared utter a contrary word, but endured silently the long speeches he was wont to make when he tried to get a point across.

Used only to the caressing love of her mother and the companionship of her brothers and sisters, the child Lydia soon learned to avoid him. Days went by when she saw him only at meal time. Meals were served in the dark heavily furnished dining room where a shadow of gloom seemed always to be hovering around the table. At each meal the pastor would enlarge upon his good intentions in taking the child in. Mrs. Lembke, as if to make up for the hardness in her husband, would say a kind word to Lydia whenever she could. She would tell her how much she wanted a child of her own but the Lord had never given her that blessing.

The first days of adjustment were very hard for Lydia. She was soon to learn the bitter taste of life among strangers. Her last thoughts as she went to bed were of her mother and loved ones. So were also her first thoughts upon awakening. She wondered how long she would be parted from her dear ones, and then the tears which she tried so hard to suppress would flow again. Lieschen was her one consolation. She was so natural, so solid, so easy to talk to and sympathetic. No wonder she found herself more often in the kitchen with Lieschen than anywhere else.

Lieschen would take her to the cowshed to get the milk and how she enjoyed watching the milking. Country life and the animal life connected with it were strange to Lydia. Lieschen would also take her to the market square to do the shopping once a week—an outing she did not like to miss for anything.

The news of the strange child at the manse spread through the village like wildfire, and all the children were anxious to see her.

### The Pastor Rehearses

Every day at breakfast the Pastor had one new rule for Lydia. These rules he expected to be kept religiously by this child of six, whose bewildered mind and cowed spirit simply could not take in all he said. There was to be strict silence in the whole house on the day before the Lord's Day when he prepared his two sermons. Nothing short of a fire could bring him out of his study on Saturdays.

For several days a week Herr Lembke would remind her of this rule. Then on Saturday morning about 10 o'clock a sonorous and pretentious voice would thunder out in measured cadences platitudes which little Lydia was soon to know so well. Her heart sank within her. This would go on for hours at a stretch and even Brutus who would always lie stretched out in the upstairs hall, tired of that intoning "pastoral" voice, would get up, shake himself, and stalk downstairs.

### Gifts for the Pastor

Lydia loved best to sit in the kitchen and watch the peasants come to the back door with heavy baskets on their backs bringing various kinds of food, their own products.

There were sausages of all kinds, homemade bread, cheeses, chickens, and other country produce, all gifts for the Pastor. The sausages would be hung in the pantry "to ripen" Lydia was told. These were graded in size and kind—row upon row. There were beef sausages and pork sausages. Long ones, thin ones, short sausages and fat ones, dry ones white with age, and also fresh ones with a roseate hue. Their aroma hung heavily in the air around the pantry. Lydia thought "when could the pastor and his wife possibly eat all those sausages? There must be hundreds of them." And always the peasants came and added to the store.

Lieschen explained to the little girl, to whom such a store of food was completely strange, that it was customary when an animal was slaughtered for the pastor to receive as a gift a share of the sausages. So there was always a big supply in the pantry.

Lieschen also told her of another custom which made the little girl's eyes shine. Herr Staub, the farmer who slaughtered pigs regularly, promised when the next pig was killed, to make some sausages to measure for Lydia. What did that mean, she eagerly inquired of Lieschen. "Well, they measure you from ear to ear and make them that long." How interesting, thought the little girl, and immediately speculated by measuring with her little fingers how long that would be. "And will they be my very own?" she questioned eagerly. "May I send one to my sister Betty?" "Of course," came the prompt reply. So Lydia looked forward eagerly to the day when she would be "measured" for sausages.

There was so much new to her in this life in the country that the first days passed quickly. There was so much to see, things she had never seen or heard of before in her own circle of family life in the city.

## Frogs at the Sunday Service

The first Sunday in Roedeldorf was most memorable. Everyone arose early in the morning and tiptoed around as if there were a sick person in the house. The Pastor could be heard moving around in his room preaching a sermon aloud as he dressed. When he at last emerged he was dressed in a suit even blacker than the one he wore on a weekday. That and the stiff high collar made his appearance strike terror into the child's heart.

At the breakfast table a long Psalm was intoned before the

meal began, which on an empty stomach was quite an ordeal. After that the meal proceeded in utter silence. Toward
the end of the meal, the Pastor said, "Lydia, my child, I
want you to sit very still through the service and set an example to the other small children who are always wriggling
around in their seats, as if they had frogs creeping up their
legs."

"Frogs creeping up their legs," thought Lydia. How horrible! And the sentence echoed in her little head from then
on. Mrs. Lembke took her by the hand and together they
crossed the street to the church. The bells were pealing out
their beautiful song. Oh, how Lydia loved those bells! They
fascinated her from the very first.

She had been introduced to the bell ringer the day before,
a youth of about 17, by the name of Johannes, and she was
thrilled to meet face to face the person who could make
those bells play so beautifully. "Would it be possible" she
had whispered to Johannes, "for me to come up into the
tower to watch you ring the bells? I would stand very still,"
she added. But immediately the expression on the youth's
face had changed to concern. "Never ask me that again," he
said, "you are too little to go up to the tower. It's dangerous."
She was thinking of this conversation when she noticed they
had reached their pew in the church, and the Pastor looking
more serious and austere than ever trooped out in his pastoral gown and regalia, followed by the choir boys in white.
Accustomed to the simplicity of "the Brethren," this ceremony was so new to Lydia. There had been none of that in
Kassel in "the meeting with the Brethren." It had all been
so plain and homelike.

And then the Pastor started intoning all that he had rehearsed so meticulously the day before. The child's thoughts
wandered off into dreamland, land of freedom and glorious
independence. Suddenly she heard another voice. It was the
Pastor's voice, but soft whispering in her ear, as if from a
distance—"As if they had frogs creeping up their legs." She
sat up quickly and felt her legs and knees to reassure herself that no frogs had entered the church to torment her. She
told herself she must sit still, the Pastor had impressed it
upon her. Yet the thought of the frogs kept returning and she
found herself fidgeting and moving from side to side. After
a while she actually could feel cold clammy frogs creeping

up her legs, and with tear-filled eyes she struggled to keep still. Why did the Pastor have to tell her about frogs, she thought. She would have sat still if he had not mentioned frogs. Frogs belonged in the brook, not in the church, and anyway why was the service so long and drawn out.

Everything was so different in this church and so cold. The big church echoed with the Pastor's voice. The ceiling was so high, and the stone walls so cold. Lydia suddenly looked up to the ceiling. There nestled above some rafters she could make out the shape of the bells. How exciting! And from then to the end of the service her eyes were fixed on the domed ceiling of the church.

After the service there was much curtsying to be done before many people. Mrs. Lembke had rehearsed the curtsy with her the day before, and remarked how well she curtsied. That pleased the child. The last parishioners gone, the church was locked up, and the Pastor and his family returned to the manse.

### "Lydia, I want to see you in my study"

At the dinner table the Pastor said in a stern voice, "I want to see you in my study after dinner, Lydia." And that was the first of many study interviews which the child was never to forget. The Pastor went to the study and five minutes later Mrs. Lembke with sadness in her face, which Lydia could not understand, told her to go up. The child, although only six years of age, sensed tension in the air as she entered the room for the first time.

It was a book-lined room, elegantly furnished in heavy black oak with a very large desk. The Pastor started right away in a low earnest voice. He reminded Lydia of what he had told her before church. She was to sit still, but to his horror (and his voice was getting louder and louder) she had behaved just like the other children. She fidgeted in her seat and instead of keeping her eyes on him, she looked at the ceiling of the church, dreaming.

Such behaviour he would not tolerate. And he would have her know this. By that time his voice was getting increasingly violent, until in a crescendo he banged his fist on the desk. He gripped the child by the shoulders and gave her a hard shake. Lydia was so taken by surprise that she could utter no sound. Her big brown eyes filled with tears. She loosed herself from his grasp and rushed from the room. In panic she fled upstairs to the attic and into the arms of Lieschen who drew her into her room and tried to comfort her. "Next time you misbehave, my child, you will get 'Hiebe' " (a spanking), Herr Lembke called after her.

The child trembled in terror. She could not remember her dear mother ever being cross with her. She was frightened, terribly afraid of this man in black, with the big voice.

Like a trapped animal she looked around fearfully. When Lieschen coaxed her to lie on the bed and try to rest, she gladly consented, for those big warm arms that embraced her were such a comfort.

## Chapter Fourteen

# The Misguided Guardian

### "If that ever happens again"

THAT night little Lydia cried herself to sleep, her little heart burdened and torn betwixt fear and longing for the comforting presence of her mother. When she awoke next morning she discovered to her horror that she had had an accident in the night. To make it more tragic, the Pastor himself had to discover it. As she was too frightened to leave her room, Herr Lembke himself came up for her.

Then the storm broke. He flung angry questions at her like a top-sergeant: one, two, three. "Will this ever happen again?" If so, he would have to apply the whip. He would not tolerate an untrained child. His voice rose in staccato tones and he snapped out, "If that happens again, my child, (He never forgot the 'my child') I will have to use one of Brutus' whips on you." With that he left the dry-eyed, terror-stricken child alone.

For the rest of the day she was banished, left with her tangle of thoughts and bewildered emotions. Only at 5 o'clock in the afternoon was the maid permitted to bring her some supper, but nothing to drink.

The following day the Pastor very seriously proceeded to tell her that her mother would probably never return to claim her little daughter. Therefore the best and kindest thing they could possibly do for Lydia would be to adopt her legally, so that she could stay with them forever. But of course, he added, he would have to teach her "how to be a lady" and not to have "any accidents." Little did Mr. Lembke know what a nervous reaction his brusque and harsh manner had on the child, and how fear alone was the cause of this new trouble. The child was frightened and feared to fall asleep. She tried to hold her eyes open with her fingers. But sheer exhaustion would finally overcome the distressed child and sleep descend on her harassed little body.

Mrs. Lembke though sorry for the child, apparently had nothing to say at all in this or any other matter. So she kept her peace and suffered in silence.

## Little Lydia Whipped

At the next invitation to the study, that formidable black room, the Pastor used one of the bulldog whips to impress on the child the terrible crime she had committed. And all her imploring that she could not help it, try as she might, was in vain. Big-bosomed and big-hearted Lieschen suffered with the child. All her senses were outraged by the harsh treatment and the indignities which the little girl had to suffer. She had grown to love her and tried whenever possible to shield her.

## The Pea Soup with Bacon

The episode with the fatty soup was indelibly imprinted on the child's mind. She had never been able to tolerate any kind of fatty meat. She had a definite aversion against it and Yente had never tried to force it on her. Therefore when a dish of pea soup was placed before her which contained "Grieben," pieces of fat pork (a favorite dish in Germany) she gagged and could not eat it. As a punishment Lydia was sent to her room without supper. But when morning came the same soup was heated and placed before her for breakfast. Again she tried, but could not eat it. At dinner and supper the same soup appeared on the table. Try as she might it just would not go down the child's throat—she gagged. By that time she was getting terribly hungry, yet could not eat the thick fatty stuff, made more repulsive with every heating up. She missed eight consecutive meals. But in the end the gnawing hunger was too much for her to bear. When two days later the same soup was set before her, she swallowed the concoction without even realizing what it was. Hunger is a cruel sensation and can play odd tricks with a human being.

The child's nervousness increased with every punishment. She was not getting used to the whippings with the dog leash. On the contrary it hurt more and more.

The farmer who promised to measure her for a sausage, actually killed a pig and gave Lydia a fine smoked sausage measuring her from ear to ear. When she triumphantly came home with her trophy the Pastor told her that as the war would in all probability last a long time, they would have to store up all the sausages. As a result Lydia never did get to taste the special custom made sausage. All this confused and frustrated the child. It made her timid and shy. She only wished to creep to her room and just be alone.

### Brutus Protests

Usually Brutus, the faithful beast, with that uncanny instinct given to some dogs, could sense the loneliness of the child and her grief, and would follow her around and stay with her in her room. He wanted to say "I love you and will keep you company." Little Lydia reciprocated the dog's love and oftentimes she would hug the big unsightly bulldog. Many a time Lieschen would find them both asleep on the rug in front of the bed.

When punishments were meted out and the child wept bitterly, calling for her mother, the Pastor would say, "The more you call for your mother, the more I'll whip you. Your mother is not coming for you. She doesn't want you and we will keep you here." This terrified the child so much that she wept for hours at a time and then Brutus would lie on the threshold of her door and whine his doggish protest against human cruelty.

### "All God's children ought to have shoes"

Lydia had one pair of shoes and they were wearing out rapidly. The Pastor had promised her a new pair for Christmas, and that meant being measured at the village shoemaker. Lydia looked forward to having a new pair of shoes almost as much as to seeing her sister Elizabeth, who was living with a family in Kassel. This too she had been promised faithfully as a Christmas gift.

Lydia would spend hours outside the shoemaker's little store, pressing her nose to the window pane, watching the shoemaker's deft fingers as they fashioned shoes—large shoes, medium-sized ones, and best of all small children's shoes. All the large shoes and medium-sized ones were of one color— black like her own. But the small shoes fascinated her most of all. They were just the kind of shoes that would fit her own little feet, and they were in different colors, brown for winter and even white ones for summer. Oh how she craved for a pair of new shoes, even if they were just black.

And then one day she found the shoemaker wielding a piece of red leather into the darlingest pair of shoes she had ever seen. Big tears rolled down her cheeks as she hurried home to tell Lieschen what she had seen. Lieschen assured her that come Christmas, Lydia was sure to get a pair of shoes, maybe not red because they were so expensive, but they were sure to be brown. How proud she would be to go to Kassel to see her sister Elizabeth and her brothers in her nice new brown shoes.

## Joy and Disappointment

A few days before Christmas thick heavy snow came down. The pastor hired a sled with two horses with tinkling bells around their strong shiny necks. Lydia happily was surprised to be invited to go along for the ride. What an unexpected treat! She enjoyed it to the full. But there was an unexpected catch to the treat, a bitter price to pay for an hour of enjoyment. On their way home from the ride the pastor told her that he and his wife would be spending Christmas in Kassel but could not take her along to see Elizabeth as they had promised. The sled ride was an effort to make it up to her.

When Lieschen saw how grieved and disappointed the child was, she offered to take her home with her. She lived in a neighboring village and had a big family of brothers and sisters and they would spend a wonderful Christmas together. This being a very practical solution (for they would save food if the house were shut up altogether for a few days) the pastor readily agreed.

But what about the shoes? Oh there was no time for them now, said Herr Lembke. They would have to wait till after Christmas. And so the child's dreams of new shoes never materialized. By spring the soles of her shoes wore away almost completely.

Christmas in Lieschen's humble home was wonderful. Everybody welcomed her and what lovely gifts they gave her—two handkerchiefs, one hair ribbon and even a small purse with five pfennigs (cents) in it. She treasured that purse for many years after. For the first time since she was parted from her mother she felt really happy and when she crept into the big bed that night with Lieschen, she snuggled up to her and fell asleep peacefully, all tension and fear gone.

## Herr Lembke Becomes a Schoolmaster

The next three months dragged wearily by for little Lydia. The pastor enrolled her in the village school where two young men taught the children. But no sooner did school start after Christmas, than both teachers were called up for military service. The village was left without a teacher. And so Herr Pastor Lembke stepped in and taught in their place. For Lydia this meant an added strain. Now there was no escape for her from the overpowering and terrifying presence of Herr Lembke. At home and at school the hard and harsh pastor overshadowed her life.

She could not understand why Herr Lembke was so entirely different from the good preacher Sommer. Maybe, she thought, these two preachers belong to a different religion and serve two different "gods". Herr Pastor Lembke's God seemed to be severe and exacting, a stickler for order and formality. Even the prayers offered to Him had to be rhythmic, sonorous and in big high-sounding words.

Herr Prediger Sommer's God was different, a friendly kindly God to whom you could speak just like you would to your own father. This was the God with whom her mommie was familiar. This was the God she prayed to when alone in the darkness and frightened. But why did they call their God by the same name, "Lieber Herr Jesus!"?

Dreary day after day, and wearisome week after week dragged on. There was no news from mother. A fiery wall of war separated mother and child. As for her brothers and sisters, they were scattered among strange people in Kassel and neighborhood, and Lydia hardly had an opportunity to see them.

## Chapter Fifteen

# Children Adrift

YENTE'S oldest daughter Elizabeth was placed in Kassel with Pastor Lembke's brother Johann Albert Lembke, a dentist, who lived with his mother and family in a spacious second floor apartment which included the dental offices.

Elizabeth at fourteen was serious beyond her age. Always mother's helper, she never had time for play nor to enjoy normal childhood. Now in the dentist's home she was allotted a small bedroom near the kitchen and told "her duties". She was to clean the dentist's office and wash the breakfast dishes every morning before leaving for school. After school she was to help with the other domestic chores. Usually her breakfast consisted of two slices of coarse rye bread and a scraping of margarine with a cup of "Ersatz" (substitute) coffee.

### Ernest

In one respect she considered herself fortunate. Her brother Ernest attended the same school as she did, enabling them to see each other daily. This brought Elizabeth both comfort and distress because Ernest's position was even worse than her own. The Schneider's with whom Ernest made his home were poor working people and although kindly disposed toward Ernest, they had little themselves. Hunger shone through his big eyes, and his gangling emaciated body gave conclusive evidence of his plight. Often cold and hungry he was hardly in a condition to concentrate on his school work. Elizabeth decided to share her piece of bread with her brother, concealing her own slice in the top of her stocking until recess time came. Then she would hand it to him surreptitiously on the playground.

Poor Elizabeth grieved for her younger brothers and sisters, especially for little Lydia who had always clung to her big sister. Her next younger brother, Jacob, was billeted with people outside of Kassel and she knew little how he fared. That too worried her.

When evening came, Elizabeth served supper to the family in the dining room. Then she was given a scant meal in the kitchen, mostly a little soup or stew and a slice of bread. After that she was sent off to her duties—scrubbing the floor, cleaning the windows, and polishing the household silver. Even in cold weather she was expected to clean the windows in icy cold water, which caused her hands to chap and to bleed.

## Otto the Odious

But what really filled her cup with bitterness was Mr. Lembke's only son Otto, fourteen years of age. An only child he was spoiled and took grim pleasure in mistreating Elizabeth. He called her "the unwanted Jewess". His misdirected patriotic instincts caused him to see in the unfortunate 14 year old girl an enemy spy. These names spread around among the children, and life at school became unbearable. Since mother left last August, about five months ago, nobody had heard from her. Was she safe? Did she join daddy in England? These were tormenting questions. Elizabeth's eyes were often red and swollen.

Whenever she and Ernest could get together on the playground, they would hold serious conversation as to what was to become of them all. They seldom heard from brother Jacob and when he did write his letters were so full of woe and grief for his mother, sisters and brother. Oh the anguish of it all! The weeks and months rolled by. It was almost Christmas by now and the chances of being reunited with mother grew slimmer.

Vivacious and pretty little Marie was the only one in good hands, always the fortunate one of the family. In Prediger Sommer's home, she was treated like their own child, the darling of the family. If anything, they spoiled her thoroughly. She was the only one who was well-fed, well-clothed, and happy.

## An Overheard Conversation

One day toward Christmas Elizabeth eating in the kitchen as usual, overheard a conversation in the dining room between the "old lady" (as everyone called old Mrs. Lembke, the dentist's mother) and a visitor. It centered around the Sitenhof children. Elizabeth was all ears. The man was saying, "How much longer can the authorities be put off? The food situation is getting worse and worse for the German people. How could the Germans be expected to waste food on these alien children? 'Die fuenf fremde Fresser!' (five foreign devourers). I will try to get an extension for them this time, but it will be difficult. Were it not for the Major, the children would certainly not be allowed to stay one day longer."

The visitor went on. "Why hadn't the mother communicated with them through neutral channels, when she had promised that she would set heaven and earth in motion on her arrival in England to get the children out of Germany?" And so on and so forth, the conversation ran on. The contemptuous description of her precious brothers and sisters as "Fressers" sent through Elizabeth's heart hot tears of humiliation which blinded her eyes.

## A Joyless Christmas

Christmas drew near. What high hopes Elizabeth had for this Christmas. When her mother left early in August, she was sure that by Christmas all the children would be re-united with mother and father as one family. Now hope faded, and grief increased. Everybody, adults and children alike, seemed to become less friendly toward them and sometimes downright hostile. War, short rations, loss of loved ones, strained nerves, made everybody irritable. What were these alien children doing in Germany anyway? Why didn't they go to Russia where they belonged in the first place?

More work, hard work, was heaped upon Elizabeth. There was no time left for her to do her homework. Consequently she got into trouble at school. Otto was becoming more abusive in speech and behaviour, while his parents took no notice of it. Her cup of grief was full and running over. Then Elizabeth conceived the idea of running away.

In desperation she went to see Prediger Sommer to unburden her heart to him and good Mrs. Sommer. Elizabeth wept bitterly as she told of the months of cruel treatment and the inadequate food. The Sommers wept with the child. She also told of the snatches of conversation she had overheard about the "Sitenhof children", and how the suspense of waiting for news from her mother was becoming unbearable. Could Mr. Sommer not do something, she implored? Perhaps he could see the Major about it.

"Dear Elizabeth," said Prediger Sommer, "there is not a

day that I do not try to contact your mother, but this is impossible. We are at war with England and contact is out of the question. I am running the danger of being branded as a spy," he concluded. He had personally stood security for all five children to the German authorities. "Hold on, my dear child. Do not be discouraged. The Lord will open the way for you to be united again with your parents." He comforted her, prayed with her and gave her some money with which to buy extra food when hungry.

"Hold on," he begged her repeatedly, "and in the meantime I will explore all channels to see if contact cannot be made."

Christmas for Elizabeth meant extra work and waiting on the family. The boy Otto by now was a nightmare to her. Before getting into bed she would sit in front of her window, watch the street lights, and dream about the time when the family would be together again. Where might her mother be now? How she prayed for her every night and morning and during the day while scrubbing the floors on her knees. She recalled the events of the last three years and the struggle her brave mother had to keep the children fed and clothed.

Yet not all her memories were unhappy ones. There were also sweet recollections comforting and soothing. She remembered the picnics on the Brusselsberg in Kassel when the laughter and frolicking of the children made her mother so glad. Oh, for those delicious big sandwiches they used to eat, stacks of them. They were made with butter or drippings and sometimes even a few slices of "wurst", that flavorsome sausage, in between. How good it had tasted. Suddenly she realized how hungry she was. That very day her ration had been cut again. At dinner she was given a small plate instead of a dinner plate, and she did not get so many potatoes as previously.

At Christmas Pastor Lembke and his wife arrived from Roedeldorf to join his brother's family, leaving Lydia with the maid. How Elizabeth hoped and longed to see her little sister! She swallowed the hot tears of disappointment and managed to ask for some news about Lydia. At once she sensed an unsympathetic attitude, which burdened her heart even more. She heard the pastor complain bitterly about how "untrained" the child was, but that in time he hoped to "remedy" that. He sounded so cruel, so much like his brother the dentist and his nephew Otto.

Next day Herr Lembke told Elizabeth, "I am breaking the news gently to Lydia that she will have to get used to the fact of never seeing her mother again, and that we will adopt her legally as soon as possible." How could the man say such wicked things in cold blood, she thought.

## All Is Not Well on the Western Front

January and February dragged on. The news from the western front did not look good for Germany. The initial advantage which the Germans achieved by violating Belgium's neutrality at the start of the war, and which promised quick victory over France, gradually petered out. It became a war of attrition.

The battles on the Marne and at Ypres stalemated the German war machine. The heavy-booted German army could march no farther. They had to dig in the endlessly muddy trenches in the numbing cold of winter across the fields of France and Flanders. It chilled the soldiers' bones and dampened their spirits. How long would it last? What would be the outcome? The only hopeful sign from the German viewpoint was on the Eastern front. There the poorly equipped and disastrously generaled Russian armies were crumbling under the onslaught of the better disciplined and organized German forces of his Imperial and Royal Majesty, Wilhelm II. But in the West, the storm was gathering against Germany. England, slow to make a start, was mobilizing her forces and rolling up her sleeves in earnest.

France was galvanized into patriotic fervor with the cry, "They shall not pass." Even the exiled Albert, King of the Belgians, was encouraging his people to resistance against the brutal aggressor.

Short rations, hunger, and general weariness were beginning to tell on the German people.

## The Lightning Rod

By a peculiar quirk of the human mind somehow the five Sitenhof children became a lightning rod which carried off some of the pent up hatreds, frustrations and disappointments of some of the Germans. Five hostages of fate, Elizabeth, of course, felt it most keenly. The care for her younger brothers and sisters and the uncertainty about her mother weighed down her narrow shoulders. The sad eyes of Elizabeth telegraphed to all who could see, the grief and anguish of a fourteen year old cast in the role of a mother.

One day Prediger Sommer called on Doctor Lembke and told the dentist that the German Government was anxious to deport all five children to Russia, "where they belonged" as they put it. Mr. Sommer urged the doctor and his wife that as Christians they should make a stand together with him and protest vigorously against such an outrageous plan. Prediger Sommer reminded them that they had promised to keep the children until their mother could fetch them, and they owed it not only to her, but to God to keep their word. But his plea was given a very cold reception. Then and there he realized that he could count only on his own efforts, and that the Lembkes would not co-operate with him. On the contrary they would be happy to be relieved of the responsibility of Elizabeth. "Of course," they said, "if she would be permitted to stay as their permanent maid, we would look upon it in a different light!"

## Secret Plans

Early in April came the long-expected message from the Major requesting Mr. Sommer to see him at 6 p.m. that day. On arriving at the Major's office, which was heavily guarded, Mr. Sommer was beckoned into an inner chamber. An air of secrecy pervaded the room, and in the twilight Mr. Sommer could sense the tension which surrounded this noble man of God who had such a responsible position in the service of his country.

"Brother Sommer," he started, "I have explored every possibility of getting these children, who carry Russian identification papers, out of this country legally, but regret to say everything has failed. It cannot be done. We are at war, and no civilian can leave the country, whoever they may be."

"But," he went on, the muscles of his strong face twitching in determination, "these children must be reunited with their mother, whatever the cost. So I have devised a plan, which, if it works, and with the Lord's help it will, is the only way I can see. It is a risk, a great risk, but are we, as Christians, to shun risks in the service of the Lord? Soldiers are courageous in battle. This is a battle of the most paramount importance to the bravest woman I have ever met. I have prayed about this for the last four weeks, and although

I cannot yet see the successful end, I know and am persuaded that this woman's faith will not go unrewarded. Somehow God's hand will guide, and this family will be reunited soon—very soon."

Prediger Sommer sat in absolute silence, deeply stirred by the pathos of the drama developing before his very eyes. Before he had time to express himself, the telephone rang. The Major answered, and Mr. Sommer's eyes continued to be fixed on that manly face, in which strength of character and goodness were chiseled by the Master Craftsman, the Christ whom he served. Mr. Sommer followed almost breathlessly the play of the facial muscles and the flicker of the Major's eyes. What was he saying? Nothing audible, but Mr. Sommer knew instinctively that the voice at the other end had called in connection with the very subject which had brought him to the Major's office.

"No," the Major answered rapidly, almost as if giving orders to a battalion of men in the front lines, clip and clear, "the five children are my responsibility. They will not be deported, but they will be escorted if go they must, and I will arrange the escort myself. It will be to a neutral European country and not to Siberia, via Norway and Sweden. I am responsible and will account for them to the highest authority. That telegram should never have been sent. Send another correcting it in a courteous way."

What could it mean, wondered Mr. Sommer, bewildered at the sudden shaping of events. The Major turned to him. "Prediger Sommer, all is well. The Lord has answered our prayers. Get the children together. They leave Kassel on the morning of April 7th. It is the deadline which the German Government has set. Do you know of a responsible woman who could act as escort?" Immediately Aunt Bess came into his mind, and he told the Major how interested she was in the welfare of the children. "Settled," said the Major with an air of finality. "The children leave with Aunt Bess on April 7th. You have three days in which to get them ready. I will arrange all details by then." They shook hands and parted, Prediger Sommer walking as if on air with a magnificat in his heart, praising God's wondrous doings. "He made a path through the sea, that the children of Israel might pass with dry feet." Somewhere from the subconscious storeroom of memory this passage floated to the surface of his soul.

From then on things moved fast. Elizabeth sobbed and

cried uncontrollably upon hearing the good news. It was as if the dams which held back her grief and anxiety suddenly gave way to the onrushing waves of relief and joy. The thought of seeing her baby sister Lydia and Jacob, both of whom she had not seen for seven months, the prospect of being reunited with her parents, was almost too much for her. She was, however, kept in the dark as to details. Nobody ever told her what their destination was, but trusting as children are, and knowing how much faith her dear mother had in Prediger Sommer, she just knew everything would be all right. She smiled again for the first time since her mother left, and sang while she scrubbed the floors. There was little she had to prepare for the journey for she had only two dresses, one change of underwear, a worn jacket, and the one pair of shoes she was wearing which she had worn day in and day out for seven months. The "old lady", Mr. Lembke's mother, had had the shoes repaired once during that time as a birthday gift, but now they were very thin all over. But what did this matter! There was a rainbow in her sky and at the end of the rainbow was the lovely face of mother.

## Chapter Sixteen

# There Were Giants in Those Days

IN LONDON city in the heart of Jewish Whitechapel there stands a four-story house, bearing the inscription in Hebrew and in English, "The Hebrew Christian Testimony to Israel." Numerous Bible passages in English and Yiddish on the walls make it clear to the passerby that this is a Jewish Mission.

The house itself looks weather-worn and old. From the street a flight of stone steps leads into a fairly large hall, where since the year 1893 Jewish people from many parts of Europe have been accustomed to foregather. To these people this place has become a spiritual haven, a home in a strange land, indeed far more so than their own cheerless overcrowded homes ever could be.

"The Hebrew Christian Testimony to Israel" was founded by David Baron who was born in Russian Poland in 1855. In time the unknown Jewish lad from an obscure town on the eastern crest of Poland, became one of the most distinguished names in Christendom. Somebody alluding to his name punned, "David Baron of the house of David, a prince." And so he was—slight of build yet a giant in spirit nonetheless. A man of God-given wisdom and charm, of great Scriptural learning, a contemporary apostle to the Jews. Above all, David Baron was a man skilled in the art of prayer.

Born in an orthodox Jewish home in Poland, the intelligent boy was to become a great rabbi.

Weary of Czarist oppression and anti-Semitism, young David together with his brother-in-law conceived the idea of emigrating to America. But when they got as far as Berlin, a pickpocket deprived David of the means to continue his journey, and David Baron came to England instead. There in the city of Hull for the first time in his life through the reading of a New Testament given to him by a Jewish missionary, he came in touch with the Messiah Jesus. David felt impelled to follow the irresistible Jesus.

His father hearing of his son's conversion was heartbroken and he addressed a pathetic letter to "My lost son, David."

### "Weep not, my father."

Eleven years later they were to meet again—the man, who in the meantime had become a flaming witness for the Messiah, and the aged father now on the threshold of the grave. Their meeting took place on the border of Russia and Germany, whither David Baron went to meet his old father. They fell into each other's arms and wept. With his father was also David's sister, who, seeing the affection and devotion of her brother, said: "Weep not, father. Surely there is something that we do not understand. He does not look as if he had no fear of God in his heart, and the fact that he has come from such a distance to see you, proves that he still has love for his father, which he would not have if he were a Meshumed (an apostate)."

Father and son communed together in the things of God until the Sabbath drew nigh. Reluctantly the elder Baron had to return across the border into Russia in order not to break the sacredness of the Sabbath. Tears flowing down his cheeks he said: "My son, I see that you serve the one God, the God of our fathers. It will prolong my life to have seen you and to be assured of this."

David Baron received his commission from his Master, "Go and tell my brethren," and David obeyed. Of all the great sons of Israel who ever witnessed for their Messiah, David was among the greatest. Like another Paul he travelled through the length and breadth of Great Britain and Europe, and even to the deserted and desolate Palestine, witnessing to his Jewish brethren, seeking to open for them a new understanding of God's plan in the light of Christ.

In this high calling Mrs. Baron, a devoted English Christian, was heart and soul with her husband. In 1892 the Barons returned to England from Palestine after Mrs. Baron was stricken with an illness as a result of the unsanitary conditions prevailing in those days in the Holy Land. Up to that time Mr. Baron was employed by an English missionary society, but David felt the need of a testimony of believing Jews to unbelieving Jews. Thus the Hebrew Christian Testimony to Israel came into being, a movement born of prayer and anguish of soul.

One day Baron was praying before God for two thousand pounds, a large sum of money for those days (approximately $10,000). This money was needed to purchase a house to start the work of God in Whitechapel. One thousand pounds were on hand and the rest the Lord would have to provide. The money had to be available by next Saturday. This was already Monday.

On Thursday morning a letter arrived from Lord Blantyre, a devoted friend of Israel, with a check for two thousand pounds, saying that he was definitely instructed of the Lord to send this money to Mr. David Baron.

## The Court of Heaven

Another incident in the life of David Baron was so characteristic of him. A Dutch lady left 10,000 gulden in her will for Mr. Baron's work. But when the will was opened after her death, as it so often happens, her relatives contested the will. Thereupon a Dutch lawyer who was the executor of the estate, wrote to Mr. Baron saying that he would be glad to undertake the defense of the legacy on behalf of Mr. Baron. Mr. Baron's reply was, "We never have recourse to earthly courts. We shall appeal only to the Heavenly court." The strange outcome however was that after two years of squabbling among themselves, the relatives decided to give the major part of the inheritance to Mr. Baron, amounting to more than double the original legacy.

## Charles A. Schoenberger and Immanuel Landsman

Closely associated with David Baron was Charles Andrew Schoenberger, a man of unusual spiritual and intellectual stature. He was born in Hungary in 1844. Early in his life Charles too came in contact with the New Testament in the home of a sick Christian friend. This led him to Christ.

In time he became a close friend of Israel Saphir, the father of the famous Jewish Christian theologian, Dr. Adolph Saphir. Eventually Charles Schoenberger became the brother-in-law of Dr. Adolph Saphir.

To further his Christian education he emigrated from Hungary to England where his unusual qualities of mind and heart, and above all his great oratorical powers attracted wide attention to him. He was offered important pastorates in different churches. But his heart was with his people, the scattered and twice destitute Jew, homeless in body and adrift spiritually.

David Baron and Charles A. Schoenberger were the founders of the Hebrew Christian Testimony to Israel.

Another man of unusual stature in this venture of the Spirit, was Immanuel Joseph Landsman, a Jewish Christian from Russia. He too was a princely man, an outstanding linguist, who could speak fluently Russian, German, Swedish, English, Yiddish, besides being a profound Hebrew scholar.

These three formed a triumvirate of spiritual pioneers, dedicated to the task of bringing Israel to Christ, and Christ to Israel. "There were giants in the earth in those days."

## Home for the Weary

It was a foggy November day when Benjamin and Yente led by a deepseated hunger for fellowship and spiritual food, came to the mission house. When they entered the mission home, Yente could feel in her throat and nostrils the sting of the fog outside which penetrated even here in the heated hall.

She looked around her and saw a group of Jews, obviously from Eastern Europe. By some small differences in dress or in manner, she could distinguish Jews from Russia or Poland, and others from Hungary, Germany or Austria. They were all sitting around a long table, most of them listening intently to a man of striking appearance.

He was rather heavyset, with gray wavy hair, high domed forehead, drooping mustache, pronounced nose, and big sad Jewish eyes—eyes which reflected endless pathos and tragic understanding. But there was a dignity about the man which somehow emphasized his "other worldliness." A spirit that was not of this world radiated from the man. She soon learned that this was Charles A. Schoenberger.

## The Prophet Ezekiel versus Dr. Ezekiel

Mr. Schoenberger was reading and expounding something from the Book of Ezekiel, as far as she could make out, and was drawing a parallel between the Prophet Ezekiel and someone, apparently a modern rabbi whom he called for the sake of emphasis and contrast, "Dr. Ezekiel"—a deadly parallel.

"Ezekiel," Mr. Schoenberger said, "came with a message from God—his heart burdened, breaking for his people, his eyes dimmed with tears because of the waywardness of his people. He could not escape the ministry which God had committed to him. It burned within him. But Dr. Ezekiel, dressed in the fine robes of the modern rabbi, was a pleasing kind of fellow. He could speak about everything under the sun—politics, book reviews, the need for betterment among the Gentiles, and of being favorable to the less fortunate Jewish brethren.

"The more fortunate brethren meantime who arrived in the synagogue in their chauffeur-driven cars listened politely. They congratulated the rabbi upon his fine speech and said they would come again sometime, business permitting.

"Ezekiel felt a personal responsibility for the souls of his people. He would pay with his own life, yes, his very own soul, if he did not speak to them the word of God. Dr. Ezekiel drowned his audience in a flood of platitudes.

"What is wrong with Israel?" he asked earnestly. "Israel is far from God because she turned away from Jesus, her Messiah. Israel and Christ belong to one another. Christ and Israel are inseparable. There is no healing, no salvation, no hope until Israel and Christ are at last united."

Such was the tenor of Mr. Schoenberger's message. His earnestness, his obvious sincerity, the pathos of his whole address which came deep from his heart, held everybody in its grip. The discourse lasted for about an hour. Then Mr. Schoenberger invited the listeners to ask questions. They sat like a transported audience. The master violinist had touched chords—unknown and unsuspected chords—in the hearts of his listeners. They sat unwilling to break the spell.

### "Why do ducks have no shoes?"

Nevertheless here and there some were frivolous and scoffing. You could recognize them right away by the little flicker of a superior smile on their faces. They knew everything. They had heard everything and cared for nothing. Yente looking at the scoffers, grieved in her heart. She remembered the words from the Gospel: "Cast not your pearls before swine." She was hurt and saddened.

"Any questions?" Mr. Schoenberger repeated.

One raggedy looking man piped up in a rather squeaky voice in Yiddish, "Preacher, I would like to ask a question." "What is it?" inquired Mr. Schoenberger. "Farvus gehn die katchkes borfes?"—Why do ducks have no shoes?

About a half dozen people giggled. However, most of the assembled were shocked by this frivolity and gave the offending man a crushing look.

"Shame on you," someone cried out. "Here is a man of God pouring out his heart before us, speaking to us in the name of God, and all you can do is try to show how smart you are. Is it any wonder that our people perish in darkness and in exile?" "That's true, that's true" a murmur went up.

Hurt to the quick and grieved in his spirit a torrent of flaming words came from Mr. Schoenberger. "He is not just an orator," thought Yente. "He is a prophet of God." Every word was like the finely balanced thrust of the sword in the hands of the master swordsman. Now he was exhorting and excoriating, stern as John the Baptist; now pleading like a father with his wayward children. Listening to him Yente thought, "Yes, there is a prophet in Israel even today."

Here in the Mission Benjamin and Yente found a home for which they had longed. When Benjamin first came back to London after his sickness during a period of missionary work in South America and was incapable of work, this mission came to his aid. Here they found friends to take a personal interest in their lives and problems. Gradually Benjamin was recovering his strength and beginning to work again. But the burning question that filled their days and nights was "When shall we see our children again?"

In the mission there was a Miss Gladys Taylor who took a particular interest in the Sitenhofs. She did everything to help them in their efforts to contact the authorities and to obtain entry permits for their children from Germany. But all efforts seemed hopeless.

Their English, especially Yente's was as yet far from adequate. In the eyes of the immigration authorities they were Russian refugees who wanted to bring to England their children still in enemy territory. How could they entertain such an idea, they asked.

One of the officers said, "Why did you not bring your children along with you? No mother leaves five children in an enemy country at such a time. We cannot help you. Go home and wait until the war is over." How could Yente explain in her broken English the complications and the unbelievable position of a Jewish refugee tossed by every tempest and circumstance.

A month of fruitless running hither and thither brought

no results. With every vain effort, the strain was mounting. At such times Miss Taylor proved herself a friend indeed. She stuck by Yente through thick and thin. She encouraged her and comforted her, and made necessary contacts for her. When Yente seemed to break down, she ministered to her physical needs, putting her back again on her feet.

And Yente prayed without ceasing: "Lord open the hearts of the right men and the right doors, so that I may have my children back with me." Nothing seemed to be able to break or daunt her. The three men of God in the mission, also the other workers encouraged her and gave her hope that with the Lord all things were possible.

Christmas, sad and dreary, came and passed. So did the month of January, spent in ceaseless but unavailing efforts.

## Inspector Strong

As an alien Yente had to report to the local police station. One day there she met the head of the alien department, Police Inspector, John Strong. Inspector Strong was a man who came up from the ranks. For years he patrolled the streets of the East End along Whitechapel Road, Commercial Road, Mile End, Petticoat Lane, and scores of narrow alleys and streets of Jewish London, a vast city in itself, teeming with bustling, brimming, almost overflowing life.

Inspector Strong was the darling of the Jewish people. A Scot himself, he could speak Yiddish like a Jew. His familiarity with the Old Testament and constant personal contact with the Jewish people, his deep love for the Lord instilled in him a real affection for the Jews. He was well aware of their weaknesses, their peculiarities, and idiosyncrasies. Sometimes he would even poke gentle fun at them. But there was love and admiration behind it. He also knew their Jewish virtues, their deep devotion and purity of family life.

Many a time he was moved by their touching loyalty and deep gratitude shown to the country of their adoption, the England which opened its doors to them when fleeing before terror and persecution. And how embarrassingly grateful they could be for just being decent and for not taking advantage of them. In the eyes of the Whitechapel Jews, Inspector Strong was a marvel. Here was a high government official who could push them around, browbeat them, take high bribes by more or less subtle methods that was common practice in Eastern Europe. But Mr. Strong did nothing of the kind. On the contrary, whenever he could he tried to help. It was their first experience of meeting a Christian not in name only. They sensed this man was something more than just a Gentile. Some of the pious, thinking in terms of the Talmud, would say, "Inspector Strong is one of the righteous of the nations of the world." But it seems folks would just pay him the highest tribute of which they were capable in saying, "Inspector Strong has 'A Yiddishe Neshome'"—a Jewish soul.

Mr. Strong was a big man with a gruff voice which often camouflaged tender feelings. Yet there was nothing soft about him or mawkish. When he saw that something wrong was being done he could be very harsh and stern until the wrong was set right.

Now after many years of service with the police, he was promoted to the position of Inspector and became the head of the Alien Department. All aliens coming to the East End of London had to pass through his office. No man knew their affairs, their fears, and their hopes, as did Inspector Strong. When he had an opportunity, and there were many, he was not ashamed to speak to his Jewish friends of the Lord Jesus, whom he loved and served. He never failed to mention that Jesus was the Messiah of the Jews.

Yente was inevitably led to this man before whom she also unburdened her heavy heart. She spoke to him half English and half Yiddish. Inspector Strong reminded her again and again that she could speak Yiddish. She did so for a while and then looking into a very Gentile face, somehow she could not bring herself to believe that a Gentile could really understand Yiddish. On she would go, telling her pathetic story as best she could in her limited and inadequate English. But her tears and anguish of soul and the pain that was written in every motion of her body, had an eloquence and effectiveness beyond words.

The Inspector did not make any promise. He only said that with God all things are possible. Then and there he suggested that they commit the whole matter to the Lord in prayer. In the privacy of his office they knelt and asked of God to open the way. Then he sent her home saying, "If I have any encouraging news I will let you know."

How people laughed at the Sitenhofs when they said they were trying to bring their five children over from Germany and they hoped to go themselves and get them. The derisive "Ha! Ha! Ha!" seemed to echo in their ears. People saw these foreigners speaking with a funny accent amidst unbelievably tangled circumstances, daring to expect the impossible. But these poor despised aliens looked beyond all impossibilities and inexorable facts. They saw God and believed Him.

## The Vicious Circle is Broken

The situation was really fantastic. They were caught in a veritable vicious circle.

The Russian Consul would not renew their travel papers unless and until the British had given them an exit permit. The British authorities on their part would not consider giving an exit permit unless the Russian Consul would extend their travelling papers. As for the entry permit for the five children into England, Yente did not even dare think about that for the time being. Sufficient unto the day was the evil thereof. When the time came the Lord would undertake.

At last about the middle of February word came from "their" Inspector as they called him now, asking Yente to appear in the Home Office. She went with Miss Taylor anticipating there would be some paper work in English. And indeed there was a long form of application given to her to fill out. Miss Taylor helped Yente to do it. Yente's heart was singing a song of praise, her feet stepping on air.

Next day another message came from Mr. Strong. This time she was to appear at the Consulate for the Netherlands in order to apply for a permit to the now neutral Holland, bordering on Germany.

It was here in the Dutch Consulate where she had been refused just this very permit over and over again. This time her heart was at ease. Her Lord was at work and who could say nay to Him?

Upon her arriving at the Consulate, she seemed to have been expected. The permit was already waiting and was given to her without delay. This was her travelling paper, which the Dutch Consul gave her in place of the Russian passport which had by now expired. With this permit she went back to the Russian Consulate who too endorsed this paper.

A few days later the message came from the Home Office

that Yente was granted an exit permit and her children permitted to enter England. All obstacles were seemingly swept away. The children were to be reunited with their parents after all. Only one problem was still to be surmounted, the important matter of transportation. Few civilian boats were crossing the Channel at the time. German submarines were lurking in the narrow waters of the English Channel and civilian traffic was almost at a standstill. But by early March 1915 passage was secured. Yente made ready to leave London for the Continent.

Yente was to meet the children on the Dutch-German border, while Benjamin would continue with his job so that they would have a home and bread when brought to London.

The evening before Yente departed, Benjamin wrote several letters in German to Christian friends, addressing them "Liebe Geschwister im Herrn" (Dear brethren in the Lord). These letters Yente was to deliver upon her arrival to the friends in Germany. Little did they imagine how incriminating such letters could turn out to be at this time of war, of wild suspicions and monstrous fears.

### "Till we meet again"

A few hours before sailing time a prayer meeting was held in the Mission. Messrs. Baron, Schoenberger, and Landsman committed Yente and her husband to the Lord before the throne of grace. In view of the danger of the undertaking, by reason of war and lurking enemy, the Lord was implored to cover His children with His mighty arm.

On March 17, 1915, Yente took her leave and said goodby to the many friends assembled in Liverpool Street Station. They sang, "God be with you till we meet again," as the train was pulling out slowly with a cling cling, and a clang clang, amidst the confusion of voices and noises of soldiers and civilians bidding fond farewells to one another. "God be with you till we meet again" rang in Yente's ear as London was melting away in the distance, swallowed by the smoke and mist of a premature spring.

She sat down in the carriage filled with soldiers. She remembered so vividly her departure from Kassel only six months ago. That time she was in the midst of German soldiers, enemies of these who were now accompanying her.

What a change! What a unique experience! If she were to tell her story, these men would be persuaded that in their midst was some fiendish spy. Whereas the truth was that she was a lone heartbroken mother led by the hand of God to a rendezvous with her precious lambs. Could anyone but God do such things? Would anyone believe her?

### Passports Please!

Shortly afterward two passport officers entered her carriage. How surprised they were to see a woman in civilian clothes among so many soldiers. Immediately they requested that she come to a separate compartment for questioning. What was she doing in that train? How did she get there? Where was her destination? These and many other questions were fired at her. She answered quietly and confidently. But her English was against her. How could she learn the language in six short months, her mind preoccupied with her children?

They could not understand her story. There were too many ramifications. Too many involvements. At Harwich there would be an official interpreter and she would be thoroughly examined. For the time being they left her alone. For the rest of the journey she prayed in her heart that the interpreter might be a man of God who would not only interpret her words but what was in her heart and help to set things right for her.

## Chapter Seventeen

# A Rough Crossing

ARRIVING at Harwich, Yente was ordered by an immigration officer to follow him. He took her to a private office and told her she would have to establish her credentials thoroughly before being permitted to embark for Holland.

An interpreter carefully questioned her, scanned her traveling permit, examined her photograph, and those of her five children. He scrutinized Yente's permit to enter Holland and appeared satisfied. The examination it seemed to Yente took endless time. She was getting anxious fearing she might miss the boat, but the officer assured her the boat sailed at midnight and that she would be in time.

### Blinding Prejudice

Just as the interpreter was handing Yente back her papers, he asked her: "With whom did you say you left your children in Germany?"

"With good Christian friends," she answered promptly.

The expression on the man's face changed rapidly. "Christian friends?" he queried.

"What do you, a Jewess, mean by 'Christian friends'?"

This unexpected change in the man's attitude astonished Yente and she suddenly realized that the official interpreter was a Jew. By now his annoyance was obvious. "How is it possible," he went on, "for a woman like you to have so-called Christian friends? Are you trying to tell me that these 'Christian friends' would be willing to keep your five children while a war is raging? Feed them, clothe them, and house them for you without compensation?"

"Woman, you don't expect me to believe you, do you?"

His manner was stern and sarcastic. He turned to the immigration officer and spoke rapidly in English. An animated conversation followed, which Yente could not understand, but the words "impossible story" and "suspicious person" seemed to be the key words of their exchange. Fear gripped her heart.

"Oh, Lord," she prayed in her heart, "give me the right

words which will convince these men of my innocence."
She was speaking. It seemed she could hear her own voice
as if far away.

"I am a Christian Jewess," she was saying. "I believe in
the Lord Jesus Christ as my Messiah, and when a Gentile
accepts the Lord Jesus Christ as Saviour, we are one in the
faith and fused together by a bond of friendship, which only
a true Christian believer can understand."

"Believe me, Sir," she continued, "I have no enemies in
Germany—only friends." This Yente said innocently—without hesitation. After she had said it, her voice seemed to
echo back at her: "No enemies in Germany—only friends.
No enemies—friends—friends. Yente there is a war on. What
have you said?"

Suddenly she realized that she should not have said this.
She felt the blood leave her body and her knees buckle
under her.

When she came to, she noticed panic-stricken, that a
clock on the wall showed 11:50 o'clock, and a woman in
uniform was leaning over her with a bottle of smelling salts.
In ten minutes the boat would sail. She stood up shakily.
From the next room appeared the interpreter. Her heart
sank within her.

"Mrs. Sitenhof," he said, "You will be permitted to embark, but the examination will be continued on the boat,
and I will come along as interpreter. If the examination
proves, as I believe it will, that you are a suspicious person,
a danger to England, you will be returned to England
tomorrow and arrested."

He said this with such finality that Yente could say nothing. She followed him quickly, praying within her soul,
"Gotteniu"—Dear Lord, take over from here on. Let us be
united together again with my little lambs, Dear Lord. Let
my testimony to this Jewish man bear fruit. Give me courage
to face the examination and may Thy will be done."

Yente felt relieved. The raging sea of fear and anxiety
suddenly subsided. Her heart was calm. "If the Lord is on
my side," she thought, "who can be against me?"

Yente was committed to a stewardess on the boat and
ushered into a small cabin. There she was undressed to her
last garment. Each garment was held to the light in search
for any possible hidden messages. Yente realized she was
being held on suspicion of being a spy. No doubt the

prejudices of the Jewish interpreter were playing a considerable part in this, she thought, but she was remarkably quiet. The Lord was with her, strengthening her. Even her long hair was let down, unplaited and examined. She was told to get dressed again.

Finally she was led to a larger cabin where four Englishmen and the same interpreter were seated waiting for her.

On the table in front of them Yente recognized her few belongings. Also all her documents and papers. She recognized on the table the two letters Benjamin had given her in which he was thanking "Die lieben Brueder" (the dear brethren) for their loving care of the children. These letters she was to hand over to the person who would no doubt escort the children to Holland. In a flash she realized how the interpreter would construe the meaning of these letters. The picture was getting darker every minute. The interpreter looked at her with unconcealed contempt.

"Woman," he said, "I do not believe your story. It will take more than this to convince me of your good intentions."

Then starting from the time she was married, Yente explained her whole story. How her husband had been disowned by his wealthy father because he had accepted the Messiah Jesus; and how after a great struggle she too had been converted and there had been great suffering ever since. "But," she added, "it has been worth it—all the persecutions and struggle. I would go through it all over again, if the Lord so willed."

Her blue eyes, dim with tears, shone with a strange light, which did not escape any of these men. The interpreter tapped his fingers nervously on the table while Yente was speaking, and when she finished, he turned on her.

"You were a traitor to your faith. You are capable of being a traitor to the country which has given you shelter."

With that he turned to the men and they went into a conference together. Presently the interpreter said to Yente, "these officers will examine you each one separately and they will then reach a conclusion."

The night dragged on endlessly. Each officer in turn questioned her through the interpreter. By the time it came to the last officer it was five o'clock in the morning. A grayish blue halflight was peering in through the cabin's porthole—a harbinger of dawn.

Yente was worn out and begged for a drink. Some water

and then tea and toast were brought to her, which revived her somewhat. The last officer was yet to interview her. He seemed to be the chief immigration officer, for he had on his uniform some insignia which the others had not.

## A Brother to the Rescue

He came straight to where she was seated, and Yente noticed, or was it her imagination, a kindly look in his eyes.

"Mrs. Sitenhof," he said, reaching out for her hand, "I want to have the honor of shaking hands with a courageous woman who loves the same Lord whom I love."

"I too am a Christian brother and naturally I am the only one who understands and believes your predicament. Not only do I believe your story and will allow you to enter Holland, but I will pray for you as you strive to regain your children. I will do all in my power to make your re-entry into this country easy."

To Yente's complete surprise he said all this in broken German completely ignoring the interpreter. Joy welled up in Yente's heart. She burst into tears and said aloud, "Lord, I thank Thee."

It was a dramatic moment, yet only the forerunner of many more to follow. The awful burden of proving that she was no spy was lifted from Yente completely. The Lord is wonderful and to be praised. The gruelling experience of five hours of questioning had left Yente limp.

Just the same, when the chief officer gave her a letter to facilitate her re-entry to England she had a song in her heart.

The boat docked at the Hook of Holland at six o'clock in the morning. The seagulls were screeching their morning devotions from the boat masts and the piers. Yente had had no sleep. Her eyes felt as if they had sand in them. But there was no time to sleep. She got together her few belongings and entered the train for Rotterdam.

There she would have to seek the help of the Russian Consul representing his Imperial Majesty, Czar Nicholas II, about getting the children out of Germany.

## Chapter Eighteen

# The Miracle of Rotterdam

IN the spring of 1915, amidst the raging of war and the booming of distant guns, neutral Holland was an oasis of comparative peace. Hedged in between France, Belgium and Germany, and the seething North Sea, her position was delicate and unenviable. Nevertheless for one reason or another her neighbors respected her neutrality.

When Belgium was overrun with the Kaiser's armies causing thousands of casualties on both sides, little Holland extended her hospital facilities to France's and Belgium's severely wounded. All trains and every available vehicle, 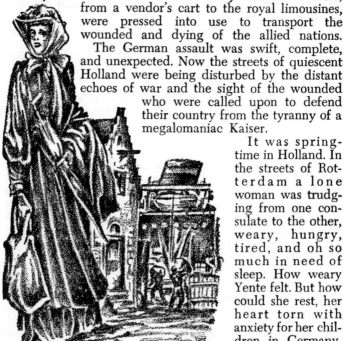 from a vendor's cart to the royal limousines, were pressed into use to transport the wounded and dying of the allied nations.

The German assault was swift, complete, and unexpected. Now the streets of quiescent Holland were being disturbed by the distant echoes of war and the sight of the wounded who were called upon to defend their country from the tyranny of a megalomaniac Kaiser.

It was springtime in Holland. In the streets of Rotterdam a lone woman was trudging from one consulate to the other, weary, hungry, tired, and oh so much in need of sleep. How weary Yente felt. But how could she rest, her heart torn with anxiety for her children in Germany, and anguished by the sight of the wounded, suffering, and distressed people all around her?

The Red Cross worked feverishly night and day. The Salvation Army headquarters where Yente had sought to make her place of refuge was pressed into service. Every bed there and like-wise the hotels and many private homes were requisitioned for the wounded.

From one lodging house to the other went Yente, sleeping here a night and there a night, and during the day pleading with the passport and consular authorities to assist her to get her children out of Germany. They seemed to think she must be unbalanced to ask an impossibility when all around was chaos and confusion.

Two weeks passed and all her feverish efforts were in vain. She had been to Amsterdam and inquired at the Russian Consul, pleading with the staff to intervene and help her. She sometimes felt swept to the edge of an abyss which threatened to engulf her. The beginning of the third week found Yente back in Rotterdam with no money, no roof over her head and no bed in which to sleep. Her eyes were swollen with weeping.

She would sit in the park and pray, "O Lord if it be thy will let this bitter cup pass from me." There was no one to whom to turn. Will there never be an end to all this misery, Yente wondered.

Her body was getting weak from lack of food. Just one cup of coffee in the early morning from the Salvation Army canteen, and on she would go, driven by some unseen relentless, superhuman force. For two nights Yente had slept on a bench in the park. By now her senses were already numb to the sensations of hunger and cold. Would nobody help her? "Lord," she cried, "help me or take me away."

## The Guardian Angel

One morning as she was stumbling through the Parklaan Street in Rotterdam, where most of the foreign consulates and the offices of the Dutch authorities were located, blinded with tears and weak-kneed from hunger and exhaustion, she suddenly became aware of running steps behind her. She hurried on, faster and faster, afraid to look around, yet knowing all the time that those footsteps were trying to catch up with her own.

"Woman, stop, stop!" she heard a man's voice behind her.

No, she must not stop, she must run.

"Why do you run, woman, why do you cry?" came the voice. "Let me speak to you, I want to help you." Overcoming the fear that gripped her thumping heart, she slowed down and turned around to come face to face with the voice. It was that of an important looking man. Authority was written all over him. Maybe he was an official who wanted to arrest her? "Let me help you," he said again. "Nobody can help me except God," Yente answered.

With that she was about ready to start running again. But the man, in a voice full of pleading, replied, "But God does not come down to earth in person. He sends His angels instead."

Yente realized that the man who followed her must be a Christian—a real believer. And suddenly her fears were gone.

All her efforts in Holland had failed. She was no nearer to reunion with her little lambs than the day when she stepped on Dutch soil. This must be the man whom God had sent to help her.

From her running she was out of breath and shaking. But now a sudden ray of sunshine entered her troubled being, and with the words "He sends His angels instead" ringing in her ears, and with tears of gratitude streaming down her face, she submitted to the gentle voice of the stranger.

"Let us go somewhere where we can talk quietly, madam," he said. "The streets are so crowded and you look tired." He was hatless and coatless as though he had departed from somewhere without any previous notice, on impulse. His dark suit reminded Yente of the many officials she had interviewed in vain during the last three weeks. He seemed to know all about her, that she had no home, no money, and that she was hungry. He led her to one of the best hotels in the city, and she followed as in a trance. Even as he entered the lobby the hotel staff bowed to him in deference. They must know him, thought Yente. Who could he be?

Now he was talking to one of the hotel employees, and turning to Yente said, "This woman will show you to a room where you can refresh yourself. In the meantime I will order something to eat in the restaurant where we will meet and talk things over."

She was too weary to even think any more. She allowed

herself to be led to a most luxurious room, such as she had never seen in her life. Upon entering she caught a glimpse of herself in the mirrored walls, and the image that confronted her made her stop short. "Can that be I?" she thought. "That pale, wan, swollen-eyed reflection over there?" She looked haggard. Her cheek bones protruding and her blue eyes, sunken and lined with dark shadows, told the story of sleeplessness and harassment.

In a moment she turned from the ghastly shadow of herself to the pleasant task before her. What a luxury to be alone in a room once more and to feel the flow of unlimited warm water. The sheer delight of the bubbly soap, the joy of feeling clean again! She who loved cleanliness so much! What tortures she had endured not to be able to keep clean! She would never forget that soul-refreshing half hour. Help in trouble, and a clean bath too! Her heart was singing and inditing a hymn of praise. "Lord, you did send an angel, you did. I know it. Thank you for sending a friend."

She came down to the restaurant refreshed. Her good Samaritan was already seated at a table for two set in a quiet corner. "Please eat first," he said, "before you tell me your story. Do you know that for days I have sat at my desk in front of the window and watched your bewildered running hither and thither in the streets. I could not settle down to work. Each day I became more restless, until today when you passed my window, I felt constrained to follow you and find out what was troubling you."

He said all this in German. Yente could see that he was a refined, cultured gentleman, soft spoken, and sympathetic. She listened on as he continued. "Let me talk while you eat," he said. The crunchy rolls and the fresh soft-boiled eggs, the sweet-smelling butter, and the variety of cheeses, together with the fragrant aroma of coffee, fairly intoxicated her. Only then did she realize how hungry she was, and remembered that she had not had a real meal for many days.

"I want you to trust me," he was saying. "Tell me what or who it is you are looking for so intently and I will, with God's help, do all in my power to help you."

Yente had expected him to tell her who he was but he did not. Yente, pouring out the fulness of her heart, told him her whole story. He listened without a single interruption, his eyes fastened intently upon her. She finished, saying,

"And then when all else had failed and the Lord had tried me almost beyond endurance, He sent you to me. This is my story."

He took out a pencil and paper and said: "I want you now, Mrs. Sitenhof, to give me all your personal data and all your documents. Now I know why I had no peace of mind at my desk. The Lord had a job for me to do. Will you stay here at this hotel for a few days, make yourself comfortable, sleep and eat and rest. I will pay for everything, so don't worry about the expense. I will get in touch with you as soon as possible.

"But please trust me. I know that your travelling papers and documents are precious to you, but without them I can do nothing. Stay here and pray that the thing which is seemingly impossible shall be made possible, for the Lord is able."

Yente was dazed by what she heard. When she answered her voice sounded far away. "May I know who you are and for whom you are working?"

"That is something I cannot tell you, Mrs. Sitenhof," he said. "It would be unwise, but I will tell you that I am in a position to help you if any man can do it. Your situation is unique and dangerous. It must be handled wisely. Do not even try to find out who I am, but commit me unto the Lord that He may direct my ways."

With that he put her precious documents, including the traveling paper with the family photograph, into his inside pocket. He bade Yente farewell, and assured her that he would communicate with her soon, perhaps in four or five days. And then he was gone. Her eyes followed him through the door and then she was left with her thoughts and stirred emotions.

A hotel hostess interrupted her reverie, and bringing more hot coffee, fresh rolls and cheese, she urged her to have a good meal and retire. She could not help crying, her tears mingling with the strong flavorsome coffee in her cup. Then she was shown to a room with a clean soft bed, with even a bathroom adjoining. She began to feel weak with emotion. Exhausted and hopeful she fell asleep.

She must have slept eighteen hours or more. When at last she woke up she was unaware of her surroundings or the immediate past. Where was she! What had happened! And then it all came back to her. No, it was not a dream.

She was awake. She had even pinched herself to make sure! She looked around carefully. What a haven of peace her room was. Everything spoke of comfort and ease. How little of these things had been her share in the past! "The Lord is good to me," she kept telling herself. "Indeed 'His mercy endureth forever.'"

## Exchange of Undiplomatic Notes

Two days had passed. Then on the third day her friend, the guardian angel, came to the hotel. His voice quivering with emotion, he told Yente to get ready for in two more days she would be reunited with her children!

Did she hear aright? Suddenly the room began to act strangely, to heave and to circle around her. Her good Samaritan, noticing her state, made her sit down while he told her of the events which had taken place since he saw her last. There was a sparkle in his eyes and he sounded also slightly amused as he related:

"At first I telegraphed the German government in your name to allow the children to travel to the Dutch frontier. Promptly they telegraphed back: 'We are shipping the five "Fressers" (gluttons) to Russia via Norway and Sweden in the next few days, unless they are taken off our hands immediately.'

"Then in my official capacity as Government attorney I wired, 'Unless you escort the five Sitenhof children safe and sound to the Dutch border by Friday of this week, the German Government will be held responsible by the Dutch Government for the welfare of these children. Mrs. Sitenhof is now under the protection of the Dutch people and unless you take good care of her children, substantial reparations will be demanded at the end of the war.'

"Upon receipt of this telegram they wired back that the children would be escorted to Sevenach near the frontier between Holland and Germany and that they would arrive by Friday."

Yente reeled! It was too much good news. Could it be really true! The "angel" who sat across the table from her was also visibly stirred—there were tears in his eyes too. Together they praised Him who delivers in time of trouble.

Now her noble friend began to outline to her all the details of procedure. First she would go to Sevenach by train. There the station master would call her name and there she would alight. The station master would then take her to his home and accommodate her over night. In the morning she would go by train, to which the station master would direct her, to the Dutch-German border. There she would be met by a man who would call her by her name.

She was to follow him and in due course her children would arrive.

Everything, he assured her, was arranged to the last detail. She need have no fear. All her needs would be taken care of.

Yente tried to speak but words seemed to fail her. She only blurted out, "Please give me your name and address so that my husband can at least write and thank you for what you have done."

But he would hear none of it. He took her hand firmly and shook it. "Sister Sitenhof," he said, "you do not need to thank me. I already have all the thanks you could give me. I can now go back to my desk in peace, knowing that the Lord has used this humble servant. I wish I could escort you myself and meet those five lovely children for whom you have shed such oceans of tears and grieved so much. But I cannot! The Lord be with you."

With that he left the room and walked out of Yente's life as suddenly and dramatically as he had entered it.

On the table were three envelopes. One containing all of Yente's documents; the second, a letter addressed to the Christian station master at Sevenach; and the third, an envelope containing six rail tickets from Sevenach to Hook of Holland, and six first class tickets on the boat for the sea crossing to England. Also in English money, ten pounds in cash, a small fortune of $50.00, to see the family home.

Such was the miracle which Yente experienced in the city of Rotterdam, and which she recalled over and over again till her dying day. It was her testimony to her Lord who never fails.

Her faith had been rewarded.

## Chapter Nineteen

# All My Children

THE five children with their escort, Aunt Bess, were scheduled to leave Kassel Station in the early hours of Sunday morning. The respective "foster parents" brought them to the station as if in secret. There was an air of secrecy hanging over all, as if spies were being smuggled over the frontier.

Pastor Friedrich Wolfgang Lembke, upon hearing that little Lydia was actually to leave his home to meet her mother, was very much put out. He did not like the idea. He still cherished hopes that he could persuade little Lydia to consent to be adopted and stay with him.

"Na," said he, the morning before the departure, "so you are going to see your mother from

England! I feel sorry for you. What a funny language she now speaks!"

With this he took down from the shelf an old English book and started reading the English words as if it were German. The result was a ridiculous mumble jumble. "That is the kind of language your Ma is speaking and they will make you talk it too. Do you still want to go there? If you had any sense you would beg me and I would let you stay in our 'Wunderschoenes Vaterland' and in our home."

But the offer held no allure for little Lydia, nor did the threat frighten her any more. What need she fear if her mother was there? Reluctantly they brought the little girl to the railroad station in Kassel the day before her departure from Germany.

Lydia's joy and excitement were boundless when she found herself once again in the loving arms of her "big sister" Elizabeth. Seven months of separation had strengthened rather than weakened the bonds of sisterly love. Betty was such a comfort to her and Lydia clung to her and followed her around every minute of the time, for fear they might be separated again. There was little said—their hearts were too full. Just to be together again, to feel the nearness of one who loved you, filled and satisfied her aching little heart.

That night Betty had whispered to her in bed that tomorrow they would be on their way to meet "Mama." It seemed a lifetime to little Lydia since she had used that wonderful word, and now she repeated it with reverence in a hushed tone, lest somebody should hear and deny her the thrill of saying it. With the word "Mama" on her lips, she fell asleep.

There was no time for breakfast the next morning. So, each taking her little bundle, Elizabeth and Lydia hurried to the station accompanied by the pastor's brother, the dentist, Herr Lembke, himself. All the way he grumbled about having to rise so early on a Sunday morning for a bunch of alien kids.

The old lady, his mother, who had made Betty work so hard before and after school for the last seven months, said her goodbyes the night before. Very ingratiatingly she shook her hand, all the while muttering how unfortunate to lose such a pleasant helper in the house, and how hard and costly it would be to replace her.

"Remember," she said, "when you go to that enemy country, England, how good we were to you, and how we shared our last crust with you, Elizabeth. I hope you will always be grateful to your German friends." To that Betty curtsied and quietly left the room, with Lydia copying her and following close on her heels.

## The Children Reunited

At the station Ernest was already there, looking thin and emaciated from lack of sufficient food. Lydia hardly knew him. She ran up to him and hugged him and tears of joy just flowed. A little way off stood Jacob, quiet and unmoved —a pathetic little boy of ten with a small bundle tied in a red cloth. When Lydia ran across to him, he dropped his bundle and almost shied away from her.

What was the matter with him, thought Betty, and going over she protectingly put her arms around him. "Ich habe Hunger" (I am hungry), he said, his big eyes looking up into hers, "und ich will die Mutter sehen" (and I want to see mother). Hunger and mother! The two words that meant more to these children than anything else in the world.

At that moment the fifth child, Marie, arrived, looking happy, well-fed and spoiled. Preacher Sommer and his wife had taken good care of her and she looked like a little rich girl beside her hungry and unhappy sisters and brothers. She was nicely dressed, had lovely brown shoes on her feet, and a new satchel slung over her shoulders. With envious eyes the other four looked her up and down. Imagine, brown shoes and practically new too! All four of them looked so shabby beside her. The uppers of their shoes were patched, the soles worn out, and their toes were protruding. In their cast-off clothing they looked so pathetic and forlorn. Elizabeth was so happy for Marie. At least one of them had had a home and real friends.

She went straight to Mr. Sommer and with hands outstretched thanked him as best she could for the loving care Marie had received in their home. Tears of gratitude welled up in her eyes. There was no time for more. Whispered goodbyes were exchanged and the children were hurried into the train.

To Lydia it seemed a journey to Fairyland had just begun. In the compartment Aunt Bess got the children together and explained how important it was for them from now on not to hold any conversations with fellow travelers, and to be as unobtrusive as possible. This was a special journey and the main thing was not to attract attention to themselves. Nobody was to be told they were meeting their mother, or where they were going.

The air of secrecy especially appealed to the boys, Ernest and Jacob. They also had so much to tell one another. Soon they withdrew to a corner and exchanged whispers for a long time. Aunt Bess produced from her basket sandwiches which were avidly consumed by all. Dear Aunt Bess did not forget weak coffee for the children (strong coffee is not good for them), and diluted milk (it goes much further). The unforgettable journey proceeded.

## At the Dutch Frontier

By evening they had reached the town of Sevenach on the Dutch frontier. As they were pulling in, the train attendant called their name and motioned them to follow him. On the platform there were some Dutch people waiting to receive them. Here was the end of the journey for Aunt Bess. A train was waiting to take her back. Marie clung to her and cried that she would not leave her. But, after being told she would see her mother the next day, she hugged her doll the tighter and resigned herself to going with the others. Jacob looked less forlorn and even smiled as he shook her hand. Ernest seemed to be enjoying the importance of it all, and kept saying to little Lydia: "Sei still" (be quiet) "Mutter kommt bald" (mother is coming soon). This only made Lydia the more excited.

The folks who met them were such lovely people. They told the children that they were to be their guests for the night. Next morning their mother would arrive. For the time being they would have to separate for the night as none could put up all five children together. So the boys would go to one home, Marie to another, and Elizabeth and Lydia to another. They did not attempt to separate Lydia from her big sister again.

A horse and buggy was waiting outside and they bundled in. Soon the boys were dropped off on the way, Marie was left with a lady, and Elizabeth and Lydia were taken by another very kind lady to her home.

What a beautiful clean house that was, thought Elizabeth. The kitchen sparkled in every corner. On the table a bowl of hot soup, sandwiches, and tall glasses of rich milk appeared, and they ate with relish. Soon they were shown to the attic and Elizabeth undressed Lydia and put her to bed. It was an unfinished attic—very large and airy. The corners and the shadows under the eaves frightened Lydia a little, but the thing that held her spellbound was the life-sized figure of a woman holding a baby in her arms.

Around her head was a halo, and the beauty of the woman and child fascinated her. She looked at the statue overawed. The lamp with which the lady of the house escorted them stood on a washstand near the figure and threw an eerie light around her. Lydia's eyes could not leave the figure. "Elizabeth," she at length was able to say,"Who is that lady and why is she here?" Elizabeth laughed, "Oh, that is a figure of the Virgin Mary and belongs to the Roman Catholics, I suppose. I don't know what it is doing in this Christian home, but I guess they found it here when they moved in and didn't know what to do with it, so they put it in the attic."

All this didn't mean a thing to little Lydia, but the figure disturbed her and she wished the lady wouldn't look at her all the time. Finally she fell asleep to dream of the meeting next day. Then she would again see mother who had left her so abruptly seven months ago, perhaps seven years ago, or was it in some previous life?

## A Day of Great Joy

Breakfast next morning in the bright Dutch kitchen was a delight. Such a selection of cheeses the girls had never seen, let alone tasted! The fresh home-made bread, sweet butter, and good rich milk tasted better to them than any meal they had had in Germany for the past seven months. Little Lydia hoped the meal would never end, and that the lady would keep on offering her more of everything. She could think of nothing else, except that she wished her dear mother could enjoy some too! Elizabeth hurried her and cut short her desire to continue the meal indefinitely, saying that mother might get there before they arrived, and that would never do.

With a hug and a kiss for each, the kind Dutch lady wiped a tear quickly from her eyes, and escorted them to a waiting buggy. There already seated were Ernest and Jacob. They too were eager to tell of the wonderful breakfast they had

had, and still smacked their lips at the thought. Today they were in high spirits. This was the day! The day they had dreamed of these seven long months!

At the station Marie and her host were waiting for the others and Marie was beaming with pride when she showed the gift of a stuffed toy dog which her host had given her. Marie! Always getting gifts, she was everybody's golden-haired darling!

Little Lydia looked enviously at the toy, but soon everything else was forgotten as they were led to a waiting room to await the great arrival of mother. Those last 20 minutes were endless. The boys played a game counting out the seconds on the big station clock, and Marie and Lydia vied with each other as to what they would say first to their mother.

Lydia was sure of her words. First of all she would ask mother why she went away for such a long time, and then tell her how much she would like a satchel like the one Marie had. She would tell her that she needed shoes badly too, her toes were almost through. But this could really wait —perhaps Santa Claus would bring a pair at Christmas anyway. If only she could have a satchel!

Elizabeth rose at last—her excitement concealed as much as a fourteen year old can—and taking Lydia by the hand started walking quickly. Her keyed up senses had detected the sound of an incoming train. From where they stood they were able to see a heavy frontier chain stretched across the platform. At that moment a train came into view. It was slowing down. Now it gave a lurch and stopped.

## Mother!

The next minute Elizabeth heard the station master call "Sitenhof," and before the others were actually aware of it, she saw a figure alight—a tall, slim, dignified figure she would know anywhere—her darling mother. Letting go of Lydia's hand she leaped forward toward the figure, under the chain, with Lydia at her heels—into the arms of mother. The others followed quickly.

One by one Yente kissed her precious children, tears of joy streaming down her face. Even strangers watching the reunion took out their handkerchiefs and wept. How could anybody help crying! This haggard looking mother and eager children half crazy with joy were the symbol of a world in the throes of war, of unspeakable heartache, of separation and reunion.

It was almost too much for Yente. Her pale face with deep shadows under her eyes stood out in the sea of faces which surrounded her.

A train on the opposite platform was waiting to take them back into Holland to the boat. The sympathetic station master hurried them to the train.

The compartment which Yente and her five children were given was small but private, and here it was, as soon as the train started, that the flood of words broke. It seemed as if all the pent-up emotions of seven months, all the fears, anxieties, disappointments and frustrations of the five found an outlet. They practically fought each other as to who should first speak to mother; who should first tell her of all that had happened, while the others remained silent. But that was impossible. Keep quiet while their hearts were almost bursting with eagerness and joy?

Yente needed five pairs of ears and eyes, and hands too, in order to satisfy them all at the same time. They all yearningly clung to her; they all flung every imaginable question at her, without even waiting for an answer. They pleaded with one another for the chance to say something to mother. "Lass' mich doch nur ein Wort sagen" (let me say just one word), they remonstrated with each other.

At last Yente brought them to order. Elizabeth was to talk first, Ernest next, then Jacob, Marie and Lydia, in order of age. But it was no use. These children (at least four of them) had had no parental love for seven months, and now the eagerness to be heard over-shadowed all else and they were almost frantic to "get their say in."

What could Yente do but weep softly for joy. Out of the babble of voices she understood one thing clearly. These children had really suffered and hungered. She looked at their feet. How shabby their shoes were, excepting those of Marie. She would get them all new shoes, she thought. And, oh, how she would cook for them, and feed them! She would soon banish the pallor of their cheeks and the shadows under their eyes, telltale signs of prolonged insufficiency. Yente studied the faces of her children with infinite keenness and tenderness.

Elizabeth looked wan and tired. There was a sad depressed look in Ernest's face. Jacob was most emphatic about being hungry and did not cease telling her that. The boys looked neglected and ill clad. "But the main thing," she thought, "is that they are with me and are mine again. God has given them back to me." "Oh, Lord, how I thank thee," prayed Yente. Then she told them all to bow their heads and they prayed. She poured out her heart in thanksgiving and praise to the Lord for this miracle which had given her children back.

A hushed silence fell over them all. One by one the children became calm again. The Lord was present in their midst.

## Sailing Homeward

Now Yente told them that they were on their way to England. Soon they would be crossing the North Sea. Maybe tonight, or early next day. This prospect thrilled the boys, for the spirit of adventure had gripped them. She told them not to be loud in their conversation with one another in German after they got on the boat, for Germany was at war with Britain and the quieter they conducted themselves all the way across, the better it would be for all of them. But that was a tall order. The children could speak only German, and after being suppressed for so many months, longed to let off steam.

That night at 10 o'clock they embarked on a small Dutch passenger boat at Hook of Holland for Harwich, England.

## Chapter Twenty

# Encounter with Submarine

**Y**ENTE was amazed to discover that the boat tickets for England were first-class and that they had two adjoining cabins to themselves. Mother and the three girls occupied one cabin, and the boys were next door, sharing the cabin with two men who made much fuss over them and supplied them with big chocolate bars and other tidbits. To the boys the ship was a dream come true, and they had great plans to explore every nook and cranny the next morning.

It was fun chasing each other down the narrow winding corridors, to be free to play with a brother, and to have that wonderful feeling that loved ones are right by. Both Ernest and Jacob harbored the same thoughts. To be one family again was too wonderful for words, and every now and then the boys would put their heads through the door of their mother's cabin, just to make sure she was there.

Soon it was time to go to bed. Each boy had the privilege of the upper bunk and how they enjoyed climbing the ladder up into their beds. This was such an unexpected treat. In the next cabin Lydia and Mary, too, amid great rejoicing had the upper berths. And when mother, who had the berth below Lydia, pushed the mattress above with her hand to amuse Lydia, the little one began to cry for sheer delight and excitement. How could one little body stand all that happiness? It was only when Yente took her into her arms that little Lydia fell asleep.

## The City of God

But Yente watched and prayed. It was a night of prayer and praise. This is how the Children of Israel must have felt when they reached the Promised Land, she pondered.

Fulfillment! What a great God she had, and what a great friend He was. She felt so unworthy. The impossible, the utterly preposterous actually had happened. Here she was at last, reunited with her five children, leaving one "enemy country" to enter another country of "the enemy." What enemy, whose enemy? She had no enemy. God had such wonderful people in Germany and in England and everywhere in the world. She knew also the others, those hard, relentless, heartless people—they too were everywhere. As for Yente, she was at peace with everybody and with the whole world. But above all, she was at peace with her Lord.

She was poor and penniless, but God had nevertheless provided all her needs. She was a homeless wanderer without a country or a city. But she was certain her God would also provide a city, the one she was looking for, a city of rest and refuge, a city of God where He and those who love Him dwell. All her life she had longed for such a city. The thought came to her suddenly that this city could be anywhere in the world, that the city of God is where God dwells.

With dreams of God and His beautiful city of peace, Yente fell asleep for a few hours.

Little did she know what turmoil the next few hours had in store for her and her children.

The ship had not left the dock yet. They were to spend the hours of darkness in the Dutch harbor and leave in the small hours of the morning for the crossing to England.

Aboard the ship were people of every kind—Dutch and Red Cross officials, but mostly refugees, escaping the jaws of war and death. All had a strained look on their faces, and it seemed to her a look of dread. The crossing at a time like this was of course fraught with danger. German submarines were lurking in the North Sea in formidable numbers and often mistook neutral ships for enemy vessels and sank them without warning. All over the ship there were notices in Dutch, English, French, and German, about life boat stations and the use of life jackets.

The boys had been thrilled when they tried on the life belts and were told what to do in the event of an emergency.

Yente awoke with a start. She could not hear the engines throbbing, and looking at her watch she saw that it was 5 a.m. But soon they had started and the boat was already rocking, a sure sign that they were out of the harbor and in the North Sea.

And then Yente prayed—oh, how she prayed, pleading for safe passage for her little ones and herself and all souls aboard. The Lord was very close to her in the early hours of that morning and she felt His presence with her. She was calm and peaceful within when she ended her prayer.

By 7:30 the boys were up and dressed and the girls soon followed their brothers. When they discovered they were on the "high seas" there were shouts of joy and clapping of hands.

After Yente had inspected them to see if they had washed their hands, faces, and ears, and combed their hair, they all trooped to the dining room where breakfast was served, their first meal together for seven months! Ernest's eyes wandered, and he was just aching to explore the boat. Yente told them they would go on the top deck and get deck chairs and sit down, and that she expected them to keep within earshot. She felt she wanted to see them all the time and keep them close together.

Already they were the talk of the boat. A woman with five children who could speak only German, aboard a Dutch liner, enroute to England! It just didn't add up.

The sun was up high now and by 9 o'clock everybody seemed to be busy. Yente sat on the deck with Elizabeth next to her, while Lydia and Mary played ball nearby. The scene was so peaceful. The thought of a war raging or of submarines lurking in the briny depths around them was forgotten for the moment.

At 9:30 Jacob came up to say Ernest was lost. They had been playing together at hide and seek when Ernest disappeared and could not be found. Two sailors hurried up to Yente and confirmed Jacob's story. They had searched everywhere but without avail. The boy had disappeared.

Yente was told to stay with the children while the search was continued. By 9:45 the captain of the boat himself came to her and with a worried look told her Ernest could not be found. Her heart almost stood still. Could it be possible that he had fallen overboard? But he was a good swimmer, and surely someone would have seen or heard something.

## Enemy Submarine

Suddenly a siren sounded, shrill and loud. Whistles were blown and orders were being shouted everywhere. Now confusion reigned. Yente stood as if rooted to the spot. That could mean only one thing—an emergency! The captain from his bridge was shouting through a megaphone, giving clear, concise orders: "To your stations, all life jackets ready. Keep calm. No immediate danger. Be ready."

Submarines were near. At that moment a sailor came stumbling across the deck with her boy, Ernest, close at his heels. Where had he been? "Where did you find him?" she heard herself say, as if her voice did not belong to her. "Aft at the flag," came the quick reply.

And now there was no time for more. Ernest quickly joined his family group and with a rather shame-faced look, which pleaded for forgiveness, he busied himself with the life jackets, which were being handed to all passengers.

This was a tense moment, probably the supreme test in Yente's life. She strained her every nerve to keep cool, calm, and collected, so that the children would not panic. But she took the situation in at a glance. A German submarine had stopped the boat. Even now, while the siren and whistles were blowing, she could see the boat was slowing up and on the bridge a sailor was getting his flags ready to signal.

The captain was addressing the crew and passengers now,

"Women and children first." It seemed as if he looked in the direction of Yente and her five, who stood lined up below him.

This was a Dutch ship, he was saying, a neutral ship, and by international law could not be sunk. "But we must be prepared," he went on. All eyes scanned the water below, while life jackets were adjusted. Lifeboats were already being loosed.

A woman nearby screamed. Someone became hysterical. The siren and whistles continued their warning, and it was to Yente the five children looked—to her, the bulwark of their strength. There she stood, tall and slim with poise and dignity, calm and fearless. Then she started up the chorus:

> "Only trust Him, only trust Him
> Only trust Him now;
> He will save you, He will save you
> He will save you now."

The children joined in quietly as if hypnotized. Now they too were without fear and, placing their hands in one another's, life jackets on, they stood ready to face anything. Their mother was with them and what had they to fear?

What superhuman strength the Lord gave Yente at that critical moment! As they stood holding hands, eyes fixed on the turbulent waves below, sirens and whistles stopped, and a hush fell over the ship. It seemed as if a magnet was drawing all eyes to one spot, where slowly and silently a periscope appeared above the waves, about 100 yards from the boat. At first it looked like a stick coming through the sea, and as it got taller and taller and was moving, everybody recognized that it was the dreaded German submarine!

They held their breath when at last the deck of the submarine appeared above the surface and gave shape to the vessel. "A submarine" gasped Ernest, who had read about them and seen pictures of them. "And it is a German submarine, Mutter," he shouted excitedly in German. "Look at the flag—Schwarz, Weiss, Rot" (black, white and red).

Now there was more signalling from the bridge and the captain was shouting through the megaphone to the figure which appeared on the deck of the submarine far below the ship. Fascinated by the sight, all eyes strained and focused in that one direction. When the Dutch identity of their boat was established, they waited for further orders.

The orders came, clip and clear; "You may proceed."

It was all over! As if in unison all heaved a sigh of relief, some laughed loudly, some burst into tears, still others continued to stand and stare dazzled at the scene which had just been enacted, in which they had taken part. Slowly the submarine submerged and was lost from sight. For a while they observed awestricken the wake of the disappearing submarine.

Yente gathered her five children around her, hugged and kissed each one in turn, and bade them stay by her, as she helped them out of their life jackets.

Now she was limp. She sank into a deck chair and the children did likewise, almost stunned by the ordeal through which they had just lived.

## The Arrival in London

The remainder of the Channel crossing was uneventful. A luncheon was served just before they arrived in Harwich, England, and a spirit of expectancy pervaded the air. Again Yente warned the children that they should not speak German loudly or call to one another, but only whisper if they must speak. Just to hear someone speak the language of the enemy was to be labeled as one of them. Yente knew that next to the earning of a living, teaching the children English would be their biggest problem.

In the immigration office she produced her papers and the letter of recommendation which the kind Christian immigration official had given her on her journey out of the country. Now she had no difficulty whatsoever to re-enter England with her children.

Once settled in the train enroute to London, her thoughts flew to Benjamin. From the Liverpool Street station she would take a taxi and soon they would be home.

## Chapter Twenty-one

# Death in the Skies

### London

THREE years is a long time in the life of a six year old. It was three years since Benjamin Sitenhof left his family for Buenos Aires, and the younger children could scarcely remember him, especially Lydia, the youngest.

Thus, when Yente led the children up the narrow staircase of the house where Benjamin and she had been living in the East End of London and pre-

sented them to their father, Lydia shrank away as from a stranger.

Through tired eyes Benjamin looked at his family. Since Yente's departure he had been sick and remained in his room in prayer for them day and night. Now the Lord had brought them all together again.

In the dimly lit overcrowded room he sat up in his bed and looked from one to the other in silence. It was almost too much to comprehend. The miracle that had taken place overwhelmed him, and he burst into tears. Now the torrent broke all barriers in earnest.

Seven forlorn souls were brought together again at last. Each sad face bore the stamp of suffering, anguish and hunger. Mary who had least to weep about, for she had been well taken care of and had suffered naught, wept the loudest! But all the past anguish, the agonized waiting, climaxing in this happy reunion, was bound to have an emotional outlet. Tears provided a happy release.

There was only one double bed in the room. "Where will the children sleep?" Yente asked. Benjamin put her mind at rest. The attic had been prepared for them for the night. Miss Gladys Taylor had found an apartment for them and had gathered together a few pieces of household furniture from kind donors and friends. At least they would have beds to sleep in. "What did anything else matter?" Yente reflected.

## Russia Square Building

In the East End of London there is a section called Cambridge Heath in Bethnal Green, populated chiefly by dock laborers, brewery hands, road workers, and such like. This section which has a radius of about two miles gets "hotter" the closer you come to the heart of it. The habitations are big tenement houses, dark, dreary, dismal four or five story buildings, where crowds of grimy, unkempt children play, scream or cry.

In 1915 these buildings were inhabited by many drunkards and their families. Anyone who could earn any kind of a living and did not spend it on drink would not tolerate the place for longer than absolutely necessary and moved away, at least to the outskirts of the section.

In the heart of this rather dismal part of London stood Russia Square Building. There on the ground floor an apartment was found for the Sitenhofs.

London was already preparing for German bombings. Sirens were being put into action to give air raid alarms. The police had special constables engaged to stand by, to keep order and see that everyone took cover. There was talk of Zeppelins coming over to blast London off the face of the earth.

And with all this going on, the Sitenhofs with their five children, who spoke only the language of the enemy (German), were moved into their new "home." The beds which had been donated were carefully disinfected by Yente, and every piece of furniture was washed clean. After Yente was through, the apartment sparkled as it had probably never done since it was built.

The curious neighbors spoke not one word to them. As for Yente, being unable to speak English and knowing the hostility of the mob to anything German, she instructed the children not to open their mouths until they could speak some English.

That first night after they moved in, the raids began. At 6.30 p.m. Benjamin had come home carrying on his back a collapsible organ which he had picked up at an old curiosity shop for sixpence and by 7:30 he had assembled it and was playing a hymn. The children were already in bed—the three girls in one, the two boys in another. As Benjamin played they sat up in bed with big questioning eyes, unable to understand how such a small instrument could play such a beautiful melody.

Their father was so clever, mother told them, he could do anything from building a house to repairing old instruments. He had always had a violin, they remembered. Now it all came back to them, how in Kassel, Germany, he used to play for them and always there was a little fable connected with the tune.

As he finished playing there was a sharp "rat-a-tat" at the door. Yente opened and a large man with a special constable badge on his coat entered quickly and slammed the door shut behind him. He explained quickly and in a somewhat excited voice that Inspector John Strong of the police station had sent him to warn them not to leave their flat at all that night, or any night after dark. They were to lock themselves in and keep quiet. An air raid warning was about to be given as a raid was expected any time. Their position as aliens who spoke only the language of the enemy was very dangerous to say the least.

With that he was gone. Dear Inspector Strong! What a friend he was proving to be! He knew that they had moved that day as Benjamin had to change their address at the police station.

Benjamin and Yente had no inkling how dangerous was their position. Ten minutes later with a blast and a wail the sirens went off. The noise was frightening. The people from the upper stories were already pouring down the stairs. They took shelter under the stairs or pressed against the walls.

### "They Are Germans"

The mob filled the small hallways and the stairs. They pushed and cursed at one another in loud voices. Then suddenly someone remembered the new tenants and word went round as to who they were. Did anybody know anything about them? Who were they anyway? They ought to open their door and let at least the children take cover. Then someone shouted, "They are Germans. They were seen buying bread at Schmidts the German baker today. Aliens—that's what they are—and they have the best flat on the ground floor. Let's get them out. Let's break down the door." All this amidst cursing and swearing!

On the other side of the wall every word was clearly heard by Benjamin and quickly translated to Yente.

"What tragic irony," they thought. Years ago Russian murderous hatred of the Jews drove them from their native Poland to Germany. There in Germany they suffered as despised "Russians." Then faced with insane animosity, they moved heaven and earth to get out of Germany, undertaking a perilous journey to England in the midst of a raging war. They defied enemy submarines lurking at sea and death raining from the air.

And now at last in England, the land of freedom and hope, they were in danger of violence by the hands of an excited mob, incensed against everything alien, regardless of race or religion.

At that time a wave of xenophobia was sweeping the country. People with foreign names were eyed with suspicion and distrust, especially if the name happened to be German. There was a rush of Schmidts and Schneiders and

Zimmermans long established in England, to become respectable and non-suspect Smiths, Taylors, and Carpenters. Among the so-called better classes the hostility against aliens was more subtle and restrained. But on the "Russia Square Building" level, amidst the uniformed semi-literate denizens of these grimy tenements, who never moved outside the precincts of the Dock Area—to be "a furriner" was to be an enemy of "good old England."

"We are in real danger if the police do not come at once," Benjamin was saying, when a crash shook the house. It was the first bomb which fell on London in the First World War.

Screams of terror came from without—a hushed silence from within. Seven praying hearts throbbed excitedly in anxious expectation. In the hall there was a terrifying commotion. Angry people banged with their fists at the door and screamed in drunken excited tones, until the three youngest, Jacob, Mary, and Lydia, clung petrified to their parents.

Then another crash sent the mob running out into the street. That was the most dangerous place in which to be. Soon the raid was over and the all-clear signal, prolonged and penetrating, was given.

## Sister Sarah

After a few weeks of this intolerable environment amidst hostile people, Inspector Strong realized more than Benjamin and Yente themselves that it was positively dangerous for them to continue living there. He had assigned a special constable to report to him the temper of the other tenants, and the reports were not good.

So one morning he himself visited the tenement and informed Yente that he had located her sister Sarah, who was now married and living in Walthamstow. Sarah was expecting Yente and the family to go out to see her, and if possible arrange to stay with her.

As there were rumors of real trouble brewing in the building, Yente decided then and there to pack a few things in a bag, take the children and leave. Benjamin had already received a message from that ever faithful friend, Inspector Strong, where they should go after work that day. A taxi was waiting to take them the twelve or so miles out to the east suburb of London. Yente who by now was used to receiving and carrying out orders, obeyed without question.

Sarah was waiting on the doorstep of a small row home with eager anticipation. She had not seen her beloved sister for fourteen years! She had married in the interim and had a little girl of seven and a baby boy. Dear Sarah! She could not do enough for "the poor souls," her sister's children, as she busied herself here, there, and everywhere, to make them comfortable.

"Beds" had been made up everywhere. Chairs were pulled together to sleep a child. Mattresses were put under the tables for the little ones to protect them in case of an air raid. Bowls of fresh fruit stood around for the children to eat and be nourished.

Aunt Sarah and fresh fruit seemed inseparable. In the years to come Lydia always remembered her first impression of Aunt Sarah's home—a conglomeration of furniture rearranged to meet the emergency, and bowls of fresh fruit. The larger the bananas and pears, the better Aunt Sarah liked it. "Est Kinderlach"— eat little children—she would coax gently. "Fruit will make you healthy and beautiful too." The children needed very little coaxing.

Then at supper when Benjamin arrived, the surprise! Aunt Sarah had been fortunate enough to find a house to rent right around the corner, and although the rent was comparatively high, she rented it for them. High to the Sitenhofs was 15 shillings a week out of the meager 50 shillings ($12.00), which Benjamin was earning at the time.

The following morning brought the cleanup day for Yente. She had made it a principle never to set foot in any abode without first disinfecting and scrubbing every room, nook, and cranny. Only then did she feel that she could live there. Yente had a very high standard of cleanliness and took every opportunity to teach her children that "a clean life goes with a Godly life."

## "A Sword and Not Peace"

After a full day of scrubbing, putting up curtains, and preparing for the beds and tables and chairs to arrive, Yente sat up late with Sarah and talked. During the conversation Yente witnessed to her sister of the wonderful way the Lord, the Messiah of Israel, had protected her and her family, and what deep peace she had found since she believed

on the Jewish Messiah as her Saviour. This was a blow for
Sarah, and the last thing she ever expected to hear.

As soon as she could recover from the shock, she voiced
a cry of bitter disappointment and anguish. "How could
Yente become a Meshumed" she cried. "What had come
over her since they last saw each other fourteen years
ago? Was this what Benjamin had brought with him from
South America?" She sobbed and wept as if a very dear
one had just passed away. "What terrible catastrophe has
overtaken my beloved young sister?" she asked amidst
tears.

Yente tried to explain what a wonderful change and peace
had come into their lives since their conversion and how
much they depended on the Lord Jesus Christ, who had
never yet let them down. They loved the Messiah, she told
her, and would pray that Sarah too would accept Him in
due course.

The close warm sisterly relationship had received a deep
blow and never again did Sarah show the same warmth and
affection to Yente as before. She had built up a high wall
of prejudice between them, and although she still loved her
sister, yet she looked upon her as a traitor and never really
forgave her for her "change of religion."

## Death in the Sky

A couple of nights after the Sitenhofs moved into the
little row house the bombing of London started in earnest.
The Zeppelins were seen trying to cross the North Sea and
one, the Graf Zeppelin, got through. The night of the Graf
Zeppelin will ever remain in the memory of the author, for
such gruesome sights seen at the tender age of six leave an
indelible memory.

The family had gone to bed when sirens sounded and
one neighbor was waking up the other by knocking loudly
on the front door. Unaccustomed as everyone was to this
new method of destructive warfare and the confusion it
naturally created, the family scattered before they could
get organized.

There was shouting amid the dropping of bombs, and the
"ack ack" of the clumsy and inefficient anti-aircraft guns
of the First World War. Benjamin translated the shouts of
the crowds outside. "They've hit it—the zeppelin's on fire.
She will come down on the houses. Leave your homes— get

into the street." Suddenly a tremendous explosion rocked the very foundation and sent the children running after their parents, who were already at the front door to see what was happening. It sounded like hell let loose.

But listen! Now the crowd of hundreds which filled the streets was shouting, "Hurrah, hurrah, hurrah!" Looking up into the sky a scene of horror met the startled eyes. There was the pride of Germany, the Graf Zeppelin, crippled and on fire from stem to stern. Lydia watched the ghastly sight dumbfounded and in terror. Inside the Zeppelin she could see the outline of the men still strapped to their seats, burning to death. The sight of the burning staggering airship, paralyzed her. Above the roar of the crowd who were screaming incessantly "Hurrah, hurrah, hurrah!" (the only words she understood) came to her quick knowledge that here were men being burned to death, while other human beings cheered the gruesome sight.

She was confused and bewildered. Violence had been done to the soul of a little six year old girl. The crowd was jostling her hither and thither, and frightened out of her wits, little Lydia hastened back to the welcome shelter of their home, where she sobbed her heart out.

The crippled Graf Zeppelin staggered and lurched another five or six miles across the country side, then crashed at Billericay, Essex, burying the poor charred airmen up to their waists in the earth.

Later they erected a monument for the poor men who perished. But in Lydia's memory the burning Zeppelin remained a symbol of cruel inhumanity—a crowd cheering men burning to death in the sky.

## Chapter Twenty-two

# A Hebrew Christian Home

## Benjamin's Skills

IN the summer of 1915 Benjamin was employed in a factory which before the war made pianos, but which now produced airplanes, particularly the wings made of plywood, four to each plane.

It was a skilled and specialized piece of work, and Benjamin did just that. He drew up the blueprints, a most exacting job, which had to be correct to the tiniest fraction of a millimeter. He went about his work quietly and unobtrusively, saying little but working much and well. Although Benjamin's heart was in the mission field, and his desire was to preach the Gospel to his Jewish kinsmen, now that he was called upon by the government to make his contribution to the war effort, he did the work "as unto the Lord."

In the moderate climate of England his health improved considerably. The heat of South America had been more than he could stand. One of the first to pioneer in the Argentine, the Lord had blessed his three years of ministry to the Jews in Buenos Aires.

Now with a war on it was his duty to do his part for the country which had so generously received him and given refuge to his loved ones. It did not take long for his superiors to notice the difference between his performance and that of the other men. But Benjamin was a foreigner, a newly arrived alien. They could not promote him officially to a responsible position which entailed the supervision of many native born Englishmen. So the intricate work requiring superior skill was given to Benjamin almost in secret. Designs of planes were of course top secrets. Benjamin did the work, but an English co-worker was given the credit.

By nature Benjamin was a dreamer with a scholarly bent of mind. Above all he was a humble man. His supreme desire in life was to preach the Gospel and to win souls to the Lord. This desire so consumed him that ofttimes his family took a secondary place. "Woe is me if I preach not the Gospel." The seeming conflict of duties toward His Saviour and his loved ones, was one of those tragic aspects of his life, not uncommon among men of single devotion.

## Weekend with the Sitenhofs

Sunday with the Sitenhofs would usually begin Saturday afternoon, when they would all go to the East End of London to the mission headed by that illustrious man of God, David Baron. Yente would hustle and bustle around the house on Saturday morning getting everything ready for the afternoon and Sunday, the Lord's Day. So it was that Sunday for the Sitenhof family usually started at 2 o'clock on Saturday. The whole family would go by bus or tramway (trolley) to Whitechapel. There was a stir in the house when the seven of them walked into the mission and filled a whole row.

Sometimes the Sitenhofs would be almost the only visitors beside the workers of the mission. The two hours they spent there hearing the word of God expounded by such princely men as David Baron, Immanuel Landsman, and Charles Andrew Schoenberger, were a never-to-be-forgotten experience for each and every one of the children, from Elizabeth the oldest to Lydia the youngest.

After the service tea would be served upstairs in the mission house. Genial Mr. Baron, now relaxed after the meeting, would usually preside, telling amusing or interesting stories out of his vast experience. There were buttered slices of bread, jam, jelly, scones, dainty little cakes, and lots of strong hot tea with milk. This was almost a ritual which both the mission workers and the visitors enjoyed greatly—a time of real fellowship. While tea was served to the rest of the family, Benjamin often would be outside the mission handing out tracts and taking part in preaching at the "open air" meeting which followed the indoor session. It would be livelier out of doors, for the mission was located in the heart of the Jewish section, and thousands of Jews would pass by on a Saturday afternoon. They were all dressed in their Sabbath finery, strolling aimlessly past with eyes roaming here and there, watching for anything unusual to take place in which perhaps they could take part.

The sidewalk outside the mission was unusually wide, so

that there was room for many people to gather around the speaker. At the edge of the sidewalk were the vendors' stalls, selling anything from peanuts to fur coats, all shouting and offering their wares for sale. Here in Whitechapel could be seen a medley of Jews from all over the world. Whitechapel on a Saturday afternoon! As interesting a scene as you could hope to watch anywhere. Saturday evening by the time the seven Sitenhofs were bundled into an overcrowded tram (trolley) on their journey home, the younger children were exhausted, if from nothing else but the sight of such a motley crowd of people. Lydia invariably fell asleep in Benjamin's or Yente's arms.

Sunday morning they would go to worship with the Plymouth Brethren which became their church home. Here Elizabeth, Ernest, and little Lydia were baptized when they accepted the Lord Jesus Christ as their personal Saviour. The fellowship with the brethren was sweet.

The house in Walthamstow soon had to be abandoned for the same reason as the previous tenants had left it. It was overrun with beetles, black beetles, which swarmed everywhere when left alone in the house for a few hours on Saturday afternoon.

## "Ere They Call I Will Answer"

One evening on their return from the mission, Benjamin had no sooner turned his key in the lock than a humming sound greeted his ears. He quickly lit the gas jet in the hall and as he walked across the dining room a sound of crunching under foot greeted his ears. He told the family to remain outside and quickly took in the situation. The floor was black with beetles. So was all the furniture. A homemade spray with disinfectant which he always kept handy was put into action and the horrible pests scuttled away. But it took hours to clean up the mess. Sleep that night for the Sitenhofs was gone, but instead it was a night of prayer. "Lord," Benjamin and Yente pleaded, "Thou knowest our need and our means. Give us a clean house tomorrow."

The very next day a letter reached them in the mail. A Christian friend had heard that a house in nearby Leytonstone might be for rent. It was a much larger house and the owner was a Christian. Benjamin wrote to the lady, who replied that she had a buyer for the house, but seeing his need and the need of his family, she had changed her mind and would not sell it but instead rent it to them. "Before they call, I will answer."

Leytonstone is a refined suburb of London at the edge of Epping Forest. It was here in a quiet neighborhood and clean street that the Sitenhofs had their first real home. It was an old "Brownstone" style, three story, eight room house. The next seven years the Sitenhofs found much happiness there.

Strenuous conditions make children grow up much faster. At 14 Elizabeth was almost grown up. There was no going back to school for her. She willingly undertook to help her parents. And so she found work in a dressmaking establishment in the East End, which during the war years made uniforms for the army. The family was so enthusiastic that Elizabeth brought home work to do at night and taught all the others how to do it, and even Lydia at 8 had a job to do on the "bobbins" (officer's braid) as they were called. It was fun working as a family. Yente worked well, and Marie and Lydia did their best too.

It was a tedious job and the boys soon tired of it. But the girls went right on helping their big sister and mother to earn extra money for bread. Five growing children to feed and clothe was quite a proposition during the war years.

## Chemical Experiments and Magic Tricks

Soon Ernest left school and found himself a job in a laboratory of a chemical factory at Stratford. He had a bent for experimenting. Anything to do with chemistry fascinated him. His special hobby was photography. So when Yente suggested the dark cupboard under the stairs for developing his pictures, he spent more of his spare time in his "laboratory" as he called it, than anywhere else.

Jacob on the other hand loved magic. Every day he would introduce to the family one of his sleight of hand tricks.

The house had a front and back yard. The first night in their new home in Lytton Road, Benjamin brought home a little black puppy dog for the children which gladdened their hearts. This was "home" in every way. They called the puppy Prince, and he soon became the pet of the family. Then a pussy cat was added. When later on eggs became scarce, Benjamin put up some chicken coops in the back yard and a hen and twelve chicks were made welcome. With all this livestock to look after and spoil there was plenty of diversion for the children.

How Yente worked to take care of her growing children! It seemed whatever she touched was blessed. Soon her neighbors called her "Yente with the green thumb." They would bring sickly and dying plants to her and Yente would nurse them, pat them, talk to them, and soon they were alive with robust health. She planted potatoes and cabbage and in a few months she was serving them to her family. Her chickens increased. Soon she set hens herself and out of 12 eggs 12 chicks would come, not one spoiled. How wonderful life was. How good the Lord had been to them.

## Open Doors and Hearts

The door of the big house at 34 Lytton Road was always open to guests. Hebrew Christians always received a warm welcome, a good meal, and a spiritual blessing when they visited the Sitenhofs.

Among the Jewish believers who felt at home in the Sitenhof family were some young men in their twenties. They came from Poland and had no kin in England. One was a bookbinder, a quiet studious learned young intellectual who had no home, except that of the Sitenhofs. One day he plucked up courage and asked Yente whether he could live with them. So a small room on the third floor was made ready and he became as one of the family. He too did pretty well on the "bobbins" at night.

## Air Raids

By the end of 1915 the Zeppelins did not come any more. They were too slow and cumbersome and an easy mark for British guns and rifles. Now instead of Zeppelins by day and by night big lumbering airplanes would come from across the English channel. They would drop a few bombs and scurry back to France or Belgium.

These air raids became increasingly dangerous and destructive. As soon as the eerie warning of the sirens sounded the children would be brought downstairs and wrapped in blankets, for the open fireplace was the only means of heating the house. Mattresses would be put under the table or under the stairs and the family would congregate in the hall in the basement which was the living quarters. In the streets policemen and special air raid wardens would shout: "Take cover! Take cover!"

When the bombs fell, windows were invariably smashed by the blast. On two occasions it was only by the grace of God that the family was not wiped out. During the air raids, which would often last two or three hours, little Lydia who loved the Lord would put her fingers in her ears to keep out the deafening sound, and pray. Her faith was simple and she trusted in Him. There was never a demonstration of fear or panic in the child, like the little girl next door, who looked for pity all day because the bombs at night made her turn blue with fear. When Lydia ran short of words to pray she would repeat the 23d Psalm over and over again.

> "The Lord is my shepherd; I shall not
> want . . .
> Though I walk through the valley of
> the shadow of death I will fear no
> evil . . .
> Surely goodness and mercy shall follow
> me all the days of my life: and I
> will dwell in the house of the Lord
> for ever . . .
> The Lord is my shepherd . . .
> He leadeth me . . ."

## In Her Tongue the Law of Kindness

There was much for Yente to do to keep her family well-fed and happy during the war years. When chicken feed was scarce, the younger children would be sent to the market on Saturday morning to pick up the green outer leaves which were trimmed off the cabbages. They would sometimes stagger home, each with two big bags full. As a reward— an extra egg.

But Yente made time to serve the Lord. She looked for opportunities of service. The lady missionaries of the East End were always busy visiting poor and sick Jewish families, often arriving just in time to help at a childbirth and doing the most menial tasks. Yente would join them and work right along with them.

She never went empty-handed. The most welcome gift

was eggs from her own chickens, an extra blessing in the days when eggs were scarce and rationed. There was always a dozen "reserved for the needy."

Yente was especially burdened for one Jewish family by the name of Rosen who had seven children of tender age. They had attended the mission for a number of years and although the father professed his faith in the Lord, his life was no testimony. In consequence his wife and children often suffered hunger and cold.

To this poor Jewish woman Yente was a ministering angel. Knowing that Esther Rosen still insisted on Kosher cooking, Yente would make it a point when presenting one of her chickens to her, to have it killed by a "shochet," the duly ordained and authorized Jewish butcher. This meant taking the chicken alive for an hour's trolley ride to the Jewish slaughter house. Often it would be a rooster. The little fellow would generally keep the fellow-trolley passengers entertained by crowing all the way into town.

After the chicken was killed "Kosher" by the butcher, Yente would have the job of plucking and preparing it according to the Jewish ritual. This meant one hour of soaking the chicken in cold water, then salting it on every side and keeping it salted for a half hour in order that the blood might flow down freely. For the children of Israel are forbidden to eat anything that contains blood.

Then she would put the chicken in the pot to boil, roll the dough to make handmade noodles, scrub the floor, and wash the children. By that time the dinner was ready and the children waiting to be fed.

By the time Yente was through it was late and she was weary. During all these "operations" Yente would be speaking to Mrs. Esther Rosen about the Lord, trying to explain to this simple Jewish woman that He loved and cared for her.

All that the dear soul would say was, "You, Mrs. Sitenhof, are my angel. What would we do without you?" Dishes washed, the apartment spick-and-span, the children in bed, Esther kissed goodnight, Yente would at last take her leave and arrive home around midnight blessedly tired. Thus she served the Lord faithfully and with a glad heart.

## Chapter Twenty-three

# An Air Raid

IN 1916 with supplies of food becoming more limited day by day, Yente found herself more than fully occupied trying to keep her family halfway well-fed. There was a shortage of potatoes, the staple food, and margarine, to say nothing of butter.

For hours on end Yente would stand in line and many a time when at last her turn came, the supply had just run out. Disappointed and weary she would go home empty-handed. Rationing was introduced at last, although in an inadequate way. But at least there was a somewhat fairer distribution of available quantities.

As the war progressed, the air raids were more frequent and more violent. They would come over in squadrons like birds and the humming of 20 or 30 engines high in the sky would send chills down your back as you scurried to take cover. One such raid was staged on a Saturday morning when housewives were out marketing. Yente had the three girls home to do their chores while she took her place in the never-ending queues. Suddenly as if from nowhere a horde of planes was seen and heard. Police, mostly on horseback, appeared simultaneously it seemed, and galloping up and down High Street shouted instructions to the people to hurry and take cover.

Yente, frenzied at the thought of her girls being home alone, disentangled herself from the crowd and turned on her neels for home, about ten blocks away. The scene about her was one of utter con-

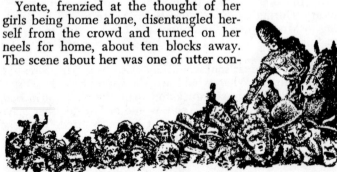

fusion. A policeman tried to grab her and push her into a doorway. But she freed herself and cried, "My children, I must get home to my children."

Now the bombs were falling in the area. At every whistle of a bomb she clutched the nearest lamp post and shut her eyes praying: "Lord bring me safely home, my children need me." At home fear gripped the three girls when they heard the whistle and "take cover," followed by the spine-chilling wailing of the sirens. Their mother out in the street! Even now maybe on her way home! They knew instinctively that she would run home to them, bombs or no bombs, and the thought frightened them more than the terrific explosions of the bombs. They stood against the wall, and amidst tears and anguished cries prayed to God for their mother's safety. This was the worst raid they had yet experienced.

Outside the anti-aircraft guns in the front of the house were shooting at the German planes. Every time a burst of shells was fired, it seemed that everything for miles around must collapse. The house rocked at its foundations.

Then out of the uproar came a cry. It reached the girls in the basement. Their mother—it was she! "Lord you have saved me—you have saved my children—I thank you." With that she collapsed at the foot of the steps at the girls' feet.

Such memories last a lifetime. They are burned into the mind and heart. Turmoil, confusion, and destruction all around, but for the true believer, there is a Shepherd who keeps His own through it all. Against such, hell itself shall not prevail.

The war dragged on interminably it seemed, leaving its mark and scars on the people. Benjamin worked hard all hours of the day and night—sometimes being sent on secret assignments for days at a time. He was thin and wan, as also was hardworking Yente. And yet there was such a peace in the home, that it seemed like an oasis in a desert place. When the family was together for the evening meal and time for evening devotions came, it seemed that the balm of Gilead was outpoured in that little home, and Jesus Christ was in their midst.

In 1918, after Benjamin was exempted from military service for the third time, due to the important government work he was doing, the hostility toward him on the part of the other men at work was reaching a point where it was not safe for him to be seen out after dark. The situation was brought to the attention of the captain in charge of the plant, who guaranteed him safety while at work, but shook his head when the question of safety after working hours was broached. But the Lord took care of Benjamin and no harm came to him.

## Armistice Day

November 11, 1918! Armistice day came as suddenly as the declaration of war had come! What a day of rejoicing and weeping for joy it was. Bonfires were kindled in the streets and fireworks were the order of the day and night, much to the delight of the younger Sitenhofs. But as soon as darkness set in, Benjamin and Yente gathered their children around the table in front of the open fireplace and the Word of God was studied and expounded by father. The Psalms were read—each child in turn—and praise and thanksgiving was offered unto the Lord, while outside the drunken crowds continued all through the night paying homage, as it were, to the devil himself, who had brought about this strife and bloodshed.

## "Let Glasgow Flourish"

Now with the War over, Ernest felt the call to prepare himself for fulltime service as a preacher of the Word of God. In 1919 he left for Glasgow where he studied three years at the Bible Training Institute, an outstanding Christian institution preparing missionaries and preachers.

That Scottish city was then a strong Evangelical center. Her motto was "Let Glasgow Flourish by the Preaching of the Gospel." Later on, however, the motto was curtailed to "Let Glasgow Flourish."

While a student, Ernest took a lively part in all Christian efforts and campaigns in Glasgow He attended street meetings and Gospel services in mission halls, throwing his heart and soul into his witness for the Lord. Of course Ernest's heart was especially among his Jewish brethren.

On Saturdays and Sundays he would attend meetings in Gorbels Cross district where most of the Jews were concentrated. Oftentimes he and others would be treated with such tokens of welcome as rotten tomatoes, tired eggs, and similar expressions of affection. Nevertheless the Lord had even among these people, seemingly impervious to the Gospel, some who were to be saved and who listened to the Word of Life and believed.

## The Free City of Danzig

The war over, Benjamin's heart and eyes again turned to the mission field. The Bolshevik Revolution in Russia was raging and he wondered what would be the outcome. Had either of his sisters and other relatives survived the bloodshed? He started praying, "Lord, there is always a great spiritual need after a war. Send me to a field of Thy choosing."

For three years Benjamin prayed for the Lord to thrust him out, so when in 1921 the Irish Presbyterian Church gave him a call to go to Danzig, he was ready.

"The Free City of Danzig" was a beautiful city of 350,000 on the Baltic Sea. Bordered by Germany on one side and Poland on the other, she had had a checkered career. A bone of contention between two rival nations it had belonged to Poland and then to Germany. The people were mostly Germans and German was the language spoken. When Germany lost the war, the League of Nations made Danzig a Free City with a Senate of its own and its own passports. As the Revolution in Russia progressed, hundreds and thousands of refugees, both Jews and Gentiles, fled through Poland to the Free City of Danzig, where they were allowed to stay, on condition they were not a burden to the State.

Many of these refugees were wealthy Jewish merchants, students and teachers, etc. The rich Jews brought with them their jewels and movable precious possessions, which they sold gradually, and managed to settle down in comfort; some starting businesses, some dealing on the stock exchange—often losing all—and some living or dying on their gambling profits or losses at the well-known Casino in nearby Zoppot, where roulette and other gambling games were allowed for all comers except Danzigers.

Then there were those refugees who were poor. The refugees of all ages it seems—the refugees who got away from the Communist revolution in Russia with their lives, but sacrificed all else—some even their families. They were a confused and bewildered motley crowd of people without homes, without food or work. Above all, they were spiritually stranded and adrift.

To these poor ones rather than to the wealthy, went Benjamin, as soon as he could get entry papers. He was peculiarly fitted to work in Danzig, for it was a work among his very

own people, whose backgrounds he knew and understood
so well. He could speak their languages—Russian, Polish,
or German. He could minister to them in a singular way.

## A Family Conference

When the call came to Benjamin, a family conference
took place. Yente and the children dreaded the thought of
once again breaking up the little home they had come by
at last with such difficulty. But seeing the light in Benjamin's
eyes, his joy and anticipation, they were caught up in the
spirit of adventure for the Lord. It was decided that Benjamin should go first, since it was difficult to obtain passports for the rest of the family so soon after the war; and
that the family should follow in a year or so after Benjamin
had established himself.

Benjamin felt the call so acutely, he did not even wait to
take out a British passport as was his right, but took a Polish
passport, much to his regret later on.

Danzig was about three days journey by train and Benjamin was stopping on the way to see David Fogel in West
Germany, his sister Dora and her family, from whom he had
not heard since 1914.

To Yente, who had moved so often and given up one
home after another, this meant just another move for the
Lord, and she would make it willingly. But what about the
children? Mary and Lydia would of course go with her.
They were too young to leave. Beautiful Betty by now was
engaged to an Englishman. She was to be married the following year. Ernest wanted to study for the ministry. Jack
was undecided what to do. By now he was working as an
apprentice in the same plant as his father and he seemed
loath to leave. So it was decided that he should stay in
England for a while and see how he would make out on his
own.

This idea of being separated from the boys grieved Yente
more than anything, for she knew how much they still needed her. And yet the call was there and she had to answer it.

The one piece of furniture the Sitenhofs hated to part
with was the piano, which had been purchased during the
war years with contributions from every member of the
family. That was the only piece that was sold, and the rest
was given away—for all it was worth. No! Things—material
things—did not fetter the Sitenhofs. They freed themselves

easily of anything that might hinder their activities for the Lord. And, strangely enough, every time the Lord provided a nicer home, each one more beautiful than the last.

Benjamin patterned his life after that of the Apostle Paul, the greatest of all missionaries. He gave not a thought to his personal comfort. He was on fire for the Lord, and his heart's desire and prayer for Israel was that they might be saved.

It has taken the author many years to grow that much in the Lord, to appreciate her father's actions and complete abandon to the Lord's will. It was the cause of some anxiety at the time. For often Benjamin would forget altogether that he had a family and with complete concentration would be "about his Father's business." It takes much growth in the spirit to understand such actions.

## Chapter Twenty-four

# Danzig, Gateway to the West

AFTER Benjamin had worked in Danzig for a year, his sense of being where the Lord wanted him, was more than confirmed. He surveyed the land, saw the low level of spiritual life and the crying need for someone to bring the message of life to the human driftwood and flotsam of that great port city. He threw himself heart and soul into the work. But it was an uphill struggle. Danzig, a city teeming with thousands of Jews, was without the Gospel message. It was uncultivated soil full of thorns and thistles. To Benjamin it was a stirring challenge.

A cosmopolitan throng crowded the streets, the hotels, the restaurants, the beaches, and the gambling places. Danzig was a "Free City" in more than one sense—a city of moral and spiritual decay.

Here freight ships from all the world docked to pick up or discharge their cargoes. Danzig, and later her rival, the newly built Polish port of Gdynia, were the links between East and West, between Russia, Poland and the rest of the world. Here the Ukrainian refugees, who in the early twenties fled the Bolshevik regime by the thousands, were "processed" before being allowed to embark as immigrants to the United States. Here they were quarantined for a time like animals, and waited their turn for shipment to the United States. Among these were many Jews.

Benjamin ministered to these in the emigration camps which were hastily set up to house them. Few had ever been out of their country before and were confused and utterly lost in the strange, bewildered cosmopolitan city. Benjamin distributed tracts and Gospels in Yiddish, Polish and German, ministering also to their physical needs wherever he could. These poor lost souls learned to love Benjamin. Some of them wept bitterly when at last their time came to leave. Several confessed Christ as their Messiah before boarding the boat.

What a sight it was to see the Ukrainian peasants and their Jewish companions board the ships with their pets and pots, frying pans, and what-have-you, flung over their shoulders, some weeping for fear of the big ocean they were to cross, some actually refusing to go at the last moment. Many took heart when Benjamin assured them that other people just like he was, who loved the Messiah Jesus, would be at the end of their journey at the pier to welcome them. The love shown them by Benjamin gave them assurance.

In September of 1922 Yente and the girls arrived in Danzig. The boys remained in England. Elizabeth, or Betty as she was called, was to return to England the following year to be married to an English farmer. Benjamin had rented a furnished apartment for his family as a temporary home. It was located on the fourth floor of a building overlooking the Danzig prison, a somber and depressing location. Every time the "Black Maria" arrived at the gates with another load of people charged with various crimes, the girls would run to the windows and observe the proceeding in tears.

Then there were the door-to-door beggars by the thousands. Most meals were shared with one or two who were hungry. They would be served on the stairs by Lydia, who delighted to feed them. She actually encouraged them to come again by saying "Auf wiedersehen" (see you again) when they left. A tract or a Gospel was handed to each one. Soon word got around in "beggar circles" and many new "customers" appeared.

## "Jerusalem" in Danzig

At that time the Irish Presbyterian Mission to the Jews decided to build a Mission house and Benjamin was asked to supervise the construction of the large five-story building, the first mission centre to the Jews in the city of Danzig. It was a time of inflation, when the currency of Danzig, the gulden, dropped daily in value. By the time a man would get his wages his pay for one day would be worth the cost of a loaf of bread. As a result laborers refused to work unless paid daily or even hourly. But even so, many lost heart. What was the use of working for money that was not worth the paper on which it was printed. "Wechselstuben," or exchange rooms as they were called, sprang up all over the city. Foreign currency, especially the English pound and the American dollar, were coveted above all else.

To the man in the street, life in Danzig was an endless battle for the next meal. Suicides were the order of the day.

Danzig became a city of sin and corruption. "Let us eat and be merry for tomorrow we die" seemed to be the spirit of the hour.

In the newly-completed Mission house which was christened "Jerusalem" many new refugees would come and receive a welcome. Most of them were young men, stranded and destitute lads between 17 and 23, who were fleeing from various countries in Eastern Europe. Many came from Poland or Russia.

Danzig was a haven to thousands of these homeless young Jews. Some of them found a refuge and the Messiah at the "Mission House Jerusalem." Here was a book store and auditorium on the first floor, apartments for missionaries on the second and third floors, and on the fourth and fifth floors a home for destitute Jewish enquirers.

In "Jerusalem" they received not only shelter and daily bread, but also the Bread of Life. They were encouraged to read the Bible and learn about the Messiah of Israel. In later years many of these people recalled with affection the blessings they had enjoyed at the Mission in the early twenties. Some of them are today themselves missionaries to their own people.

## Wedding Bells

When in the summer of 1923 Betty returned to England to get married, Yente and Lydia accompanied her. At 22, Betty was a beautiful young bride. Always quiet and often in a pensive mood, one could not penetrate her deeper feelings. She had experienced so much sadness in her young life, and so little of ease and happiness, that she was thrilled at the prospect of settling down in a home of her own in England. Her future husband was a "gentleman farmer" and cattle dealer, who came from a well-to-do Essex family of squires and landowners.

The wedding over, Yente and Lydia were heartbroken when the parting came and they had to go back to Danzig.

## Bronislava Jamaika

One of the homeless and friendless newly-converted Hebrew Christians who found her way to "The Jerusalem Mission House" in Danzig was Bronislava Jamaika, a Polish Jewess of about 30 years. Because of her faith in the Messiah, Bronislava had been completely rejected by her family.

She was welcomed into the Sitenhof household before the Mission was even officially opened and remained with them for over two years. During that time she became very attached to the family, but her favorite was the youngest daughter Lydia. Unable to find employment in her own trade as a maker of artificial flowers, Bronislava helped in the home and made herself generally useful. Rejected and expelled by her own kin she felt alone and insecure. But with Yente to befriend her and help her grow spiritually, and with two young girls Mary and Lydia to keep her stepping, she learned to laugh again and was happy.

## "My Cousin Victor"

One day when Lydia was celebrating her 16th birthday, Broni, as she was now affectionately called, told Lydia who was a very sympathetic and good listener, something about her background in Poland. She recalled how heartless her family had been to her when they discovered that she went to the Mission, and how she had lost her job in consequence. When Lydia asked Broni whether there was any other in her family who believed in the Messiah, she became dreamy-eyed and sighed. "Yes," she said, "I have a cousin of 21 years, who accepted Christ and was baptized. He is now studying at the University of Warsaw. It was through him that I first became interested in Christianity. He is such a fine young man and (another sigh) oh, how nice it would be if you could only meet him. Perhaps you might fall in love with him and marry him at some future time!"

"What is his name?" asked Lydia. "Victor" she said, "Victor Buksbazen." The conversation was soon forgotten by Lydia and the name did not even register in the young girl's mind.

Broni's dream was to spend the rest of her life with Lydia who understood her so well, and her thoughts would often dwell on any opportunity which might make it possible.

"Lydia," she would say, "when you get married I will come and live with you and take care of your family for the rest of my life."

Cousin Victor was mentioned affectionately once or twice by Broni after that, but nothing she could devise brought him any closer to Danzig.

## "Private Secretary"

The German language was one of the great handicaps with which the girls had to contend. In their childhood for five or six years they had spoken only German. But since they went to live in London only English was spoken, especially during the war years. German was soon forgotten. How quickly children learn and forget a language! Mary and Lydia now struggled to learn German again, but not hard enough. Why learn German when so many Germans and some Danzigers spoke some English or at least seemed to understand it? So many refugees planned or hoped or dreamed of going to England or America some day and tried hard to learn English. "Speak to me in English," they would say, eager to hear it spoken.

The girls' education in German was thus cut short and Lydia decided she would take a business course in shorthand and typing. But her progress was slow, not being able to understand well enough her German speaking instructor.

After six months, her business course only half completed, Lydia ventured forth and found herself a position as "Private Secretary" to a lumber exporter. This man thought it would enhance his business standing to introduce an English secretary to his customers. But his "English Secretary" could neither write German letters, nor take down dictation in English any too well, certainly not his dictation. The English vocabulary of her boss consisted chiefly of "Good morning," "Good afternoon," "Have a cup of tea," and "Good business."

The "job" turned out to be that of errand girl and no office work. Lydia was sent out in all kinds of weather. In winter it was bitterly cold, sometimes twenty degrees below freezing. She was told to take letters, messages and documents to banks, shipping houses, and customers. Sometimes she would be sent to docks to deliver shipping papers to the boats. The docks and boats fascinated her. As for Benjamin he was not too happy about Lydia going to work before completing her education. But he knew it was one of the sacrifices a missionary has to make if he wants his children with him in the field, and so held his peace.

After three months of running around in the intense cold, Lydia left this place to apply to one of the Scandinavian shipping companies. She had little practice in English shorthand, but the night before the interview, she went through her stenography textbook, and the next day with trepidation was ushered into the office of Captain Burton, an Englishman who was looking for a secretary. Lydia was so anxious to obtain this work, yet deep in her heart she knew how ill prepared she was for it.

### "Captain, Give Me a Chance"

Captain Burton looked at the slip of a girl—just 16—almost four years younger than any other girl in the big company, and smiled to himself. With long corkscrew curls dangling over her shoulders and a confident air, because she could at least speak English to the man, she grasped the pencil and pad when he said he would give her a test. However, when she tried to read back the dictation her lack of experience was evident. "Don't be discouraged little girl," Captain Burton told her. "You made a valiant effort. I like your spunk. Come back next year when you are 17 and have had a little more practice."

Her heart sank and she fought to keep back her tears. "Captain Burton," she said, "Please give me one more chance before next year. I'll come back in three days and if I fail your test, then I will wait until next year. But I am sure I shall be satisfactory." Captain Burton patted her on the shoulders and with a big grin said: "With that spirit I couldn't refuse you, but I don't for the life of me know how you will make it in three days from now."

That was the challenge Lydia needed. She flew home, got out her books and made everyone who knew any English at all, give her dictation, or at least talk to her while she wrote it down in shorthand. Then she transcribed every word as best she could. Every caller at the Mission for the next three days was pressed into service, for that job meant more to her than anything else at the time. For the next three days Lydia neither ate nor slept. But when she returned for the test on Thursday of the same week, to the amazement of the unbelieving Captain Burton, Lydia passed the test and got the position at—

### "Bergenske Baltic Transports, Ltd."

The company's headquarters was a five-story office building. Here she mingled with Danes, Norwegians, Swedes and Britishers. She could speak English all day long to her heart's desire. She learned her work quickly and became so efficient that Captain Burton who shortly after left the firm to become an independent Lloyds Agent, asked Lydia to be his secretary and work for him at a much increased salary. But nothing could tempt her to leave, not even the idea of doubling her salary. Money meant nothing to Lydia. It was the thought of travel and adventure which the shipping firm could offer that kept her there.

And travel opportunities came soon enough. By summer she was booked to go to London in a 1500 ton cargo boat loaded with timber from the Baltic States. These freighters usually carried several passengers aboard, all employees in the company offices. The pleasant trip to London of five days was a privilege reserved for valuable employees only.

# Chapter Twenty-five

# The Invisible Wall

THE free city of Danzig was definitely the crossroads of Eastern Europe. Here the immigrants would flock in order to go on to better and freer countries. Young Jewish people, unable to enter colleges and universities in their anti-Semitic homelands, would gather in Danzig, where the atmosphere was more congenial and friendly.

And so it came to pass that one day Benjamin's sister Sima of Warsaw appeared on the horizon, bringing along several of her grown sons and daughters to look around for a possibility for them to study in Danzig. Benjamin was overjoyed to see his sister, with whom he had not visited since his conversion twenty years before. His sister was married to a businessman, Mr. Aaron Goldberg, and was the mother of a large family of ten children.

Her older children were already engineers and doctors, and some of the young ones, students in the university of Warsaw. Sima was very friendly toward Benjamin. "Let us," she would say to Benjamin, "just remember that you are my brother and I am your sister and we will get along fine. Come and see us with your family in Warsaw. You will be more than welcome."

One day Benjamin went out to visit his sister and brother-in-law, Mr. Goldberg, in their cultured and comfortable home in Warsaw. Theirs was a hospitable home open to one and all, where the younger set of Jewish intelligentsia would foregather. Here was Benjamin's natural environment, comfortable, cultured and gay. The Goldbergs received Benjamin with open arms, but nevertheless before long he felt out of place. How could Benjamin feel at home where Christ was not loved? He could not help but feel the conflict between divided loyalties, between his dear ones according to the flesh and his faith.

Mary and Lydia who came along with their father to meet their cousins felt strange in this intensely Jewish atmosphere. First of all they could not understand Polish which was spoken in the home of the Goldbergs. So a smattering of German had to do as a means of understanding.

179

Into the Goldberg family, university students, doctors, engineers and ardent Zionists would come and go. Zionism among the Jews in the early twenties was in full blossom. It was the hope of Israel, persecuted, despised and discriminated against in Europe. In the Goldberg's home Zionism was the family religion.

The Sitenhof girls knew little about the Zionist movement and its strong effect upon Jewish thinking and feeling. To them the future of the Jews was the divine plan for Israel according to the Scriptures. The ardent spirit of Jewish nationalism and Zionism was strange and bewildering. The girls listened carefully and the fervent spirit of these young people would pervade their hearts. They heard the Jewish national anthem, Hatikvah, the Hope:

> So long as the Jewish heart
> Beats in a Jewish breast
> And Jewish eyes with longing gaze
> Toward Zion in the east;
> So long our Hope shall never perish
> The ancient Hope and immortal
> Yet to be a people free
> In Zion's land and in Jerusalem.

The fervent yearning and the intensity of this song could not but touch their hearts. How they longed that God might restore the Holy Land to His scattered people. A new world was opened up to them and they were caught up in the enthusiasm which their numerous cousins and friends displayed.

Lydia's mind was in a turmoil. Here she was, a faithful witness and follower of the Lord Jesus Christ. She could not help but take a stand for Him. But this was unpleasant and unwelcome to the Goldberg family. Her sister, in order not to give offense, kept quiet. But Lydia spoke up, in spite of the fact that she was told by her cousins that they were not interested and she should keep her religion to herself. This made Lydia the least popular with the cousins. They liked her and her sister all right, but they wanted none of the strange religious ideas which Lydia was so free in voicing.

It was a delicate situation with the unbelieving relatives. They wanted to enjoy the companionship of their uncle, aunt, and cousins from England. There was a mutual attraction between them and a strong barrier at the same time. Lydia often thought of the verse, "I have come to bring not peace but a sword."

In the early spring of 1925 Elizabeth who lived in England gave birth to her first-born son, little Dick. Betty's hands were full, what with her duties on the farm and to her family, and all alone without her loved ones. So she asked Lydia to come over from Danzig and stay for a while with her on the farm. Lydia was only too glad to do so.

To Lydia, England, in which she lived for the first seven years of her school life, and in which she blossomed out from childhood into young womanhood, meant home. How often she longed for her family to be back with her in England. She would pray to the Lord to bring them back somehow if He saw fit, and give her dad a mission field at home. While London itself was teeming with Jews, why could he not be a witness to them?

In her childlike faith she believed the Lord would answer her prayer. She kept busy on the farm, feeding the chickens, looking after the baby, her first nephew, and helping generally with the housework. Time passed rapidly, but she longed for her family, especially her mother.

## A Prayer Answered

Around that time the International Hebrew Christian Alliance was founded in London. The first conference was to take place in London in 1926. How great was her joy when she received a letter from Danzig that her father and mother were planning to attend the first conference. What was more, her father had accepted a call to work in London under the London City Mission. Lydia was sure the Lord had answered her prayers. A deep sense of gratitude pervaded her whole being. Thank God, now the family would be together again. No longer would the boys have to live elsewhere, but in their own home with their parents. Truly the Lord was good.

Ernest and Jack were both eager to study for the ministry. Some Christian friends from America who were guests in the newly-established Sitenhof home, urged the boys to come to America where they would have the opportunity to work their way through college. In England any kind of education was prohibitive at that time. Only the well-to-do could afford a college education.

## Off to Moody

In the spring of 1926 Ernest left for Chicago to enter
Moody Bible Institute. A few months later Jack too was on
his way to Chicago, aboard the good ship Leviathan, headed
for Moody. Yente was heavyhearted on parting with her
dear boys, but realized that it meant a future in the service
of the Lord, and she was grateful for the opportunity which
came their way.

As for Lydia, she was in her element in London. Confidently she went out to find office work. With her partial
knowledge of German she was able to get a position in
a shipping firm in London. Her sister Mary worked as a
saleslady in a store. Soon the Sitenhofs settled down to a
quiet life. Their little nephew Dick was the delight of the
whole family.

The Barbican Mission to the Jews, in London, was at
the time establishing an Enquirers Home and school in
the north of London for young Jewish converts. Benjamin
was asked to take charge. He seemed to be particularly
suited for this work. Again the family moved, this time
into a large house in the north of London. Soon the home
was filled with young men who came from all parts of
Europe as well as from the Danzig mission in Poland.
Under the able teaching of Benjamin some of them were
prepared for future training as missionaries.

The next five years were busy ones in the Sitenhof home.
When a letter came from the boys in America it was truly
a red-letter day for the whole family. They wrote cheerful
letters. They were working hard at college and maintained
themselves by doing all kinds of work between their study
periods. Jacob, the younger brother, was in turn a park
sweeper, an elevator boy, a waiter, and on occasion a
magician. Magic tricks were his specialty and he was quite
popular at commencement exercises in various schools
where he would combine his magic with a Christian message. On Sundays both Ernest and Jacob would preach in
various churches, sometimes way out in the country. In this
way they were gaining experience in the ministry.

A few years later the Enquirer Home was closed and
Benjamin worked among the Jewish people in the East End
of London, visiting, speaking in the open air, and preaching
the Gospel faithfully and untiringly.

Mary by this time had started a small gown shop and was kept busy. Lydia had worked for several firms and gained much experience in office routine. Lydia and her mother were joined together by deep affection and friendship. She knew how much her mother missed her boys and she tried to make up the loss, at least in part.

Benjamin's heart was burdened for Danzig. There were so many missionaries in London who could do his work, but few or none in Danzig. So back he went in 1931, without the backing of any mission board, trusting the Lord to provide. Lydia had a good job and was able to support Mother if necessary. The call to Danzig was so definite and irresistible that none of the family could object. His heart was on the foreign mission field. In the ensuing years he often went hungry and was unable to pay the rent for a small room. Many a time his converts would share a loaf of bread with him or a pot of soup. Material things meant little to Benjamin. He had the true spirit of the early disciples of our Saviour. He cared not for raiment, or food, or where he would sleep, but went forth in faith.

The years of stress and strain had left their marks on Yente. Now she was suffering much with rheumatism. Yet these were happy years for them. Lydia did her utmost to provide her mother with every comfort. On weekends Elizabeth would come from the farm bearing gifts, such as eggs, butter, cream and vegetables. Elizabeth's husband was an ailing man and the burden of her small family fell upon her young shoulders. But she was of the stock that weathers storms bravely. She was faithful and strong.

By now Lydia was secretary to a leather merchant in Bermondsey, London. Her boss, a German Jew, looked upon her as his good right arm. He would introduce her to customers, saying, "She says she is a Jewess who believes in the Messiah. I say she is a Goy for she does not keep our holidays. But whatever she is, I would entrust her with all I have and more, for she is faithful—the best secretary I have ever had." Her business connections gave Lydia many opportunities of witnessing to her Jewish customers. And, strangely enough, she was much respected by them as a Christian.

Ernest by this time, having been ordained in California as a minister of the Gospel, returned to England. The "unprodigal" son came home and the joy was great. He was offered the pastorship of St. Columba Church in Walthamstow, London. A year later his bride-to-be, Ella, arrived and they were married in Ernest's Church. Ella Grauer came of French-German Christian stock. Her father, David, was a pioneer who came to California before the turn of the century. He worked hard building up an orange farm and a home for his growing family, and incidentally helped transform the erstwhile wasteland of Southern California into the thriving province which it became later.

Ella was raised in a deeply Christian atmosphere and had a God-given love and burden for the Jews. As a young girl she went to the Bible Institute of Los Angeles, and during her student years worked closely with Dr. Immanuel Gittell in the Jewish Mission. It was there that she met Ernest. They soon fell in love, and were later married in London.

But now clouds, dark and angry and low hanging, were gathering over Europe and the whole world. An evil maniac by the name of Adolf Hitler came into power in Germany. Events were moving rapidly to an awesome climax.

# Chapter Twenty-six

# "The Hebrews of Hutton"

AFTER Ernest married his California bride, he and Lydia purchased for their mother a bungalow in the country. They felt it was time for Yente to have a place of her own, and truly "Whitby Moor," as they called the red brick bungalow in Hutton, Essex, was the home in which she spent the happiest years of her life.

Hutton was a peaceful hamlet removed from the noise and rush of the big city, and yet near enough for Lydia to commute to her work in London, just half an hour by the express train. In the evening Lydia would come home worn out from work, but the peace and quiet of the country was so invigorating and soothing that in the morning she felt fresh as a daisy, ready to catch the 7:22 express to London.

All those precious memories still linger on in the heart of the author. She remembers the soft twilight of those balmy summer evenings when they would sit on the veranda after a day in the city, and hear the hoot of the owl and the chirping of the cricket. When the smell of the newly-cut grass was so pungent it almost intoxicated you; when the full moon over the meadow at the end of the garden would throw a path of light directly at you; when the cows would moo in the distance, and the echo would come back at you; and the silence of the summer night would enfold you softly, and make you lift up your head to Heaven and thank Him Who made all things and made them well.

The flowers Yente grew were so varied and colorful and the lawns so green, one was reminded of a picture post-card of an old English garden with roses round the door. The sweet peas grew up the sides of the veranda in great profusion, so that their scent, mixed with that of the wallflowers which grew in abundance nearby, made one stagger at times.

In the eight years they lived at Whitby Moor nothing ever became commonplace to Lydia or her mother, nothing was ever taken for granted. Every morning the heavy dew clinging to the lawns and flowers, the scent of the carnations and roses, which greeted one's nostrils through the always open windows, thrilled them anew. Here indeed was rest and respite from the bustling world. Here Yente's dream came true.

Yente's love for flowers and the warm smile which she had for her neighbors and her love for the children, became proverbial in the hamlet. Altogether the Sitenhofs were considered a different kind of people and nicknamed not without affection, the "Hebrews of Hutton."

## The Man with the Funny Mustache Takes Over

All seemed so peaceful and happy in Whitby Moor. Yente attended to her flowers, hoed and seeded and sowed, and nursed lovingly those plants which were not doing so well, until they looked happy and smiling.

But one day, the 30th of April 1933, darkness descended upon the Jews of the world, and not only for the Jews but for all mankind. Adolf Schicklgruber Hitler became chancellor of Germany. Adolf, born in a little village on the Austrian-German border, was the son of a petty government official who up to the age of 35 went by the name of Alois Schicklgruber. Adolf, a soldier in the Austrian army in the First World War, came home embittered, unemployed and frustrated.

Germany was a defeated and humiliated nation, suffering poverty, depression, and general demoralization as a result of a lost war. As always, the Jew became the scapegoat for all frustrations and unfulfilled desires for conquest and enrichment.

The little corporal brooded over his personal and national misfortune and mingled with similar, embittered veterans. Their philosophy was a mixture of hate for democracy, for the Western Allies, and above all, the Jews. Hitler with his hysterical oratory soon became their spokesman and leader. It is one of those remarkable instances in history, where a neurotic half-crazed demagogue was able to personify and to give expression to all the secretly nurtured or openly expressed desires and hatreds of a great nation.

His half-literate book "Mein Kampf," setting forth his "Gospel" of hate and his blueprints for world conquest, was foisted upon the German people as the new Bible. Hitler, his book "Mein Kampf," and violent threats against the world in general, and the Jews in particular, were brushed aside or even laughed away as something not to be taken too seriously. When the world realized its mortal peril, it was too late.

The only statesman who in those darkling years recognized the real menace of Hitler and his gangsters was Winston Churchill. He warned England and the world of the wrath to come. But his was "a voice crying in the wilderness" of indifferent or intimidated leaders. For his pains Churchill was rebuffed and rebuked until it was too late.

Winston Churchill later was to describe Adolf as "a bloodthirsty guttersnipe, a monster of wickedness, insatiable in his lust for blood and plunder."

The men around Hitler, the Goehrings and the Goebbels, looked upon him, or pretended to believe that he was the "messiah" of the German people, a god of the ancient German Valhalla, the seat of bloodthirsty mythological deities and cruel heroes. In the words of his lieutenant and mouthpiece, Joseph Goebbels, the destiny of Hitler was "to unchain volcanic passions, to arouse outbreaks of fury, to set masses of men on the march, and to organize hate and suspicion, with ice-cold calculation."

And the man with the unruly forelock, the dark smidgeon of hair for a mustache, and the coarse hoarse voice, did exactly that. A nation entrusted her honor and future to a demon-possessed man.

His main object of hate was the Jew, whom like his predecessor Haman, he vowed to exterminate altogether. But for God, he came pretty close to achieving his satanic purpose.

Yente would sit at her radio listening to the mad rantings of this evil man who made no secret of his purpose to destroy the Jews. She suffered inwardly more than she showed. Every time she heard him speak it would be like a knife piercing her heart.

Yes! They looked for a city which hath foundations whose builder and maker is God (Hebrews 11:10). And here was a wretched man claiming to be the "savior" and "builder" of the German people. Yente would say to Lydia, "Doesn't he (Hitler) know that without God he can only lose?"

She would meditate and read her Bible daily, much troubled in spirit because of the threats which were constantly flung out to her people, in a voice venomous with hatred such as the world had never heard before. These were hard days for Yente. Her heart was torn for her brethren's plight in Germany.

## A Business Venture

Early in 1935 Lydia had tired of office work and decided to venture into another field on her own. She rented a small dress shop in Muswell Hill in the North of London and started with hardly any capital, but made good. By May of that year she was doing very well.

Having never been a saleslady, people, and Lydia herself, were amazed to discover that she had rather unusual sales ability. Within three months she established a name for herself to such a degree that the wholesalers were eager to give her credit. She was always so prompt in paying her bills.

Handy with a needle and a sewing machine, she attempted all alterations of coats, suits and dresses herself, thus saving expenses. There were no complaints. Satisfied customers came back again and again. This discovery of a "new" Lydia gave her added confidence. Her turnover increased every month by one hundred per cent.

## A Meeting with Destiny

In the Spring of 1935 Lydia was introduced to a young man at the home of a Hebrew Christian friend, Rev. Jacob Peltz, who at the time was secretary for the International Hebrew Christian Alliance in London. Lydia and her sister Mary had been invited to a Sunday afternoon tea. On seeing the young minister she remarked to her sister about how much he reminded her of Broni in Danzig! "Do you mean Bronislava Jamaika?" the young man asked. "Yes, how did you guess I meant her?" Lydia in turn inquired. "Because," he answered, "Bronislava Jamaika is my second cousin."

So here was the Victor Buksbazen dear Broni had talked about to Lydia twelve years before! How strange and inscrutable are the ways of God! Here was Broni's cousin, now a young ordained minister of the Gospel, on a deputation tour in England, serving as a missionary to the Jews in Cracow, Poland. And of all people, Lydia should meet him! Could it be other than that the hand of God was in it to bring these two young people together?

They were mutually drawn to each other. In fact, when they first saw each other they knew that something of the utmost importance had happened in their lives.

On seeing her for the second time three weeks later in her store, Victor lost no time and proposed to her. At first Lydia was not able to say definitely yes, wishing to know more clearly the Lord's will in the matter. By the time Lydia was ready to give a definite answer many things happened in the world as well as in her own life. Both she and Victor went through the shadows during that time.

There were many lessons Lydia had yet to learn before the Lord could use her. Above all, she had to stand the test of suffering and much grief. In this way the Lord prepares those He will use for His purposes. He breaks them, melts them, molds them, and when the test is over, He fills them, if they are willing, with the Holy Spirit, and uses them to glorify Him. But without the fire there can be no refining.

## Among the Jews in Old Cracow

In August of 1935, having spent three months in England, Victor Buksbazen went back to his mission station in Cracow where the Lord was using him in the Gospel witness to the Jews. Cracow was the ancient capital of Poland, with a history of one thousand years, as old as Poland herself. At the end of the eighteenth century Poland was partitioned by her three rapacious neighbors into three parts. Cracow became the main city in Austrian Poland and the stronghold of orthodox Jewry.

It was a common sight to see long-bearded Jews with side curls, dressed in fur hats and long black coats, white socks, and knee breeches, walking to or from the synagogue and places of rabbinical learning. Missionaries from England had been carrying on a Gospel witness among the Jews of Cracow for nearly a hundred years, and a number of Jews were saved. But every time after one missionary would pass away or retire, there would be a lapse of some years, and the small flock of believers would be scattered.

When Victor Buksbazen was ordained to the Gospel ministry, he was sent to revive the work in Cracow. The beginnings were very difficult and discouraging. But as in other places there were many Jews, especially among the younger generation, who were hungry spiritually and looking for food which would satisfy their souls. The preaching of the Gospel opened up a new world to them and a gate to a new life.

## Jacob's Return

Jacob Sitenhof, who spent a number of years in the United States studying at Moody Bible Institute and other Christian institutions, had by now completed his education and was ordained as a minister of the Gospel. He decided to return home to his beloved mother and to his family circle.

With him came a young friend of his by the name of Roger Derby. Both Jack and Ernest while students in America made the acquaintance of the Christian family of Mr. and Mrs. Lewis Derby of Minneapolis. The Derbys were true lovers of God's people and put their heart and soul into the cause of befriending the Jewish people, especially Christian Jews. People referred to their home as "The Hebrew Christian Hotel."

Ernest and Jacob found a true home away from home, and Mrs. Derby was a mother to them in the absence of their own mother. Now Roger, a student of music, was coming to England together with Jacob in order to continue his musical studies.

The Sitenhofs, especially Yente, were all excited at the thought of having Jacob back home again. Now her happiness would be complete with her two boys and the whole family together.

Finally the day of Jacob's return (Jack to the family) to England arrived. The whole family, excepting Benjamin still in Danzig, awaited him at Waterloo Station to greet him and his American friend Roger Derby from Minneapolis. It was nine years since they had been together and it was a joyful reunion. Yente was completely happy and her heart full of praise and thanksgiving.

This was in the early Fall of 1935. Christmas of that year was a memorable one. The whole family gathered together at Whitby Moor to celebrate the Lord's birth. The little bungalow was full to overflowing. Fires burned cheerily in the open grates of all the rooms. Hearts that were happy to be together again united in Christmas carols. The Lord was good to the Sitenhof family. The only cloud on their horizon was the one of hate for the Jewish people hanging over Europe.

Jacob was a powerful preacher—an orator for the Lord. He had studied long and hard in the United States and now he was taking a little rest and thoroughly enjoying the best home the Sitenhofs had ever had. Yente's cup was full and running over. She had both sons with her again. The future of the well-favored and popular Jacob seemed to be especially bright and promising.

"But my ways are not your ways and my thoughts are not your thoughts." When the sun smiles down on our green meadows and gardens in bloom, who would give thought to the raging storm that may soon bring grief and suffering in its wake?

## "Lydia, the Seller of Purple"

With the coming of Hitler, Jewish life and property in Germany underwent a complete devaluation. In fact these commodities lost almost all value. Those Jews who were not interned in concentration camps or murdered outright, were frantic to leave Germany. Those were days when a visa to a country outside the grasp of Hitler often meant a visa to life; its refusal, a sentence to death.

At that time a certain Jewish businessman, a merchant of printed silks and rayons, by the name of Hermann Silber, came to London with some of his capital which he managed to get out of Germany. Anxious to set himself up in business, he made contacts with his business associates, inquiring for a person who could speak German as fluently as English, and help him get established in England. Lydia Sitenhof was pointed out to him as a most trustworthy and capable person.

When Mr. Silber approached Lydia, she was unwilling to accept his offer because she was too happy in her own little business venture. But he opened his heart to her and told her how badly he needed her help. Here he was a stranger in a strange land, and unless she would be willing to help him his whole future and that of his family would be in jeopardy. Mr. Silber persisted and would not take no for an answer. He would come daily to her store and plead with her.

When Lydia said, "Herr Silber, but I do not know anything about your business or your trade," he would answer, "Aber mein liebes Fraulein, (my dear young lady) anybody with common sense can learn a trade. But character, honesty, loyalty, these are gifts of God, and He has blessed you with them."

Lydia sought guidance and finally accepted Mr. Silber's offer. He was very generous with her. He not only bought out her business, but he also offered her a more than adequate salary, in fact the highest she ever earned in her life.

Strange! Here was a Jewish man who knew that Lydia was a Jewish Christian, and yet in spite of all ingrained prejudices was willing to entrust her with his fortune and his future. Jewish people often take a negative stand against Christianity, and yet deeply appreciate the fruit of the Spirit of Christ, an unconscious tribute to the greatest Molder and Maker of character.

The next day Mr. Silber and Lydia went to a bank and opened a deposit account and rented a safe deposit box. When the manager asked Mr. Silber in whose name the bank account would be, he said: "In the name of this young lady, Miss Lydia Sitenhof." "How much do you wish to deposit?" "Five thousand pounds for a start" (the equivalent of about twenty-five thousand dollars). "Do you know her so well that you will entrust such a sum to her?" "Oh, yes," he said, "I would entrust her with everything I have."

Mr. Silber handed over to Lydia the detailed instructions of his business, instructions that were the apple of his eye, because they represented the whole basis of his future. Lydia could not help being deeply moved by such boundless confidence shown in her by a man she hardly knew. Mr. Silber had to rush back to Germany to attend to his business at the other end, but he promised to return in a week's time.

Lydia set to work with all her might. First she rented spacious offices and showrooms for the display of the goods which her boss sent over from Germany. Then she went into the details of her new duties. Every piece of silk had its basic price, transport price, custom and income factor to be worked out exactly, and the thousands of different figures had to be at her fingertips. A German calculating machine was a great help. It was a mechanical wonder, simplifying calculations in a marvelous way.

Now she had to employ a staff of travelling salesmen and office clerks. All her abilities were put to a supreme test. Mr. Silber's absence for "one week" was protracted for three months. When he came back, Lydia had the warehouse and office staff hired, the salesmen were busy getting new customers, the goods were in circulation, and the new enterprise was running smoothly—a going concern.

## Benjamin Comes Home

In the meantime Benjamin was in Danzig working among the Jewish people, and seeking to comfort and help his little flock, which was exposed to the consuming hate of the rising Nazi power. He stayed with his flock as long as he possibly could, but his days in Danzig were numbered.

One day Benjamin was ordered to leave Danzig within thirty-six hours. There was no room under Hitler for the preaching of the Gospel to the Jews. So Benjamin came to London.

By this time England had become a haven of refuge to thousands of Jews fleeing from Hitler. Refugees from Germany, Austria, and Eastern Europe were pouring in daily, escaping Hitler's clutches. These people in their suffering and bewilderment were specially open to the claims of the Gospel, their hearts hungry for friendship and compassion.

Benjamin, always eager to witness to his beloved people, began a Gospel ministry in Brighton, Sussex. Brighton on the southern coast of England within easy reach of London, was the hub of a whole cluster of seashore towns and resorts. Nearby were Hove, Worthing, Shoreham, Lancing and many others. Each had a considerable number of Jewish people, with few to tell them about a Saviour in the hour of their need.

Benjamin knew these people from his previous life and service among them in Europe. He understood them, not only because he could speak their various tongues, but also because he understood the unspoken language of their fears and woes, their hopes and yearnings. Soon Benjamin's mission in Brighton became the center of Christian witness and compassion.

## Chapter Twenty-seven

# The Isle of Man

**P**EEPING around the corner there was yet another time of trial for the Sitenhofs.

Jack was invited to come as a candidate to a Presbyterian Church in the town of Ramsey on the Isle of Man. He made an excellent impression on the congregation and they decided unanimously to extend a call to him to become their pastor. Jack liked the church. Mr. Quilliam, one of the elders of the church who was specially interested in the young pastor, took him around in his little Austin, and introduced him to the mayor of the city, and all the personalities of the Island.

It was a beautiful Island with its deep stormy bays and lovely beaches, hills and hamlets, going back to ancient days with quaint but very friendly people. From the northern tip of the Island he looked across the water and saw three ancient lands: Scotland to the north, England to the east, and on the west the Emerald Isle called Ireland.

Jack thrilled at the thought of his future ministry as pastor. He was to preach his first sermon on Good Friday. To honor the new pastor and to show him goodwill, all the churches in Ramsey decided to close and hold a joint service with Jack Sitenhof bringing the message.

Lydia, who had had a successful but hard winter, planned to spend the Easter vacation on the Isle. When she set out, the whole world looked perfect to her. The spring flowers seemed to be smiling especially at her. Life was wonderful indeed. She travelled all night, sitting upon the deck of the boat as it crossed the Irish channel on its way to the Island. Lydia was so happy for her brother's sake, and glad at the prospects of a few days rest for herself on the Isle which Jack had previously described as "a little bit of Heaven." When she left London, her employer, Mr. Silber, had begged her to take off a few days longer for a well-earned rest.

But instead of rest, grief waited to greet her. Lydia naturally expected her brother to meet the boat in Douglas, the port city and the capital of the Isle of Man. When he was nowhere to be seen, she thought not too much about it, but took her luggage and boarded the bus which was to take her to Ramsey. It was a beautiful bus ride along the coast line, high on the cliffs above the sea. It was beauty which defies description—rugged, stern, majestic. It was so breathtaking, that Lydia almost forgot to alight at the address Jack had given her.

And then a sense of foreboding filled her heart. When her hand touched the knocker of the door, she knew all was not well. Something had happened to her brother in the seven days since he had left home. At her knock, Jack came downstairs. It was only seven o'clock in the morning and he was dressed in a robe. Yet when she saw his troubled countenance, she knew that something terrible had happened and she was rooted to the spot.

Pulling herself together she was following him up to his room. Not a word had been spoken between them. Not even the greeting which Lydia had visualized so often during the night on board. It became obvious to her Jack was suffering from a nervous breakdown. Lydia spoke lovingly to him, and tried to reason with him. Even before she had taken off her coat she got down on her knees with her brother and cried to the Lord to take over. Then a calm took possession of her, a resolute calm which was the Lord's answer to her prayer. She acted fast. The day was Wednesday.

A meeting of the church session was called and another preacher for Good Friday was procured. Lydia telephoned London that she was flying back the next day with Jack. All at once in the twinkling of an eye, it seemed the world which looked so pleasant and serene the day before, became a valley of tears and grief. Lydia chartered a small plane and by noon the next day in brilliant sunlight they were winging their way back home.

"Is this a dream?" Lydia asked herself. Maybe a nightmare which will disappear just as the coastline of the Isle of Man was disappearing way down below. Perhaps she would awaken to a reality sweeter than this ghoulish presence. "Oh, Lord, do give strength, come to our aid, for there is none who can help us," Lydia prayed.

Yente's grief and heartache at the sudden turn of events was very deep. Doctors and specialists were consulted. Jack seemed to flounder amidst waves of distress. One day all would be well, but the next morning deep gloom would sweep over him and he was not himself. It was a time of grief for all the Sitenhof family. But prayers which went up for Jack were surely answered.

Lydia, who was earning more money than any of the other members of the family, gladly assumed the brunt and burden of the medical bills which piled up. Even before the darkness of sorrow had set in the Lord had provided help. What a blessing that position turned out to be for them all. No one who has not gone through the agony of waiting for a loved one to recover from such an illness can know the depths of sorrow, and sometimes of despair, which comes over you.

When a wholesome smile returned again to the friendly face of brother Jack it seemed that the Lord had smiled again upon the sorely tried family.

## Lydia's Marriage

While Jack was recovering from his illness, Victor was involved in a horse and cart accident in Poland. He was visiting some friends in the country near Cracow. As they were driving back to the city the horse took fright on the downgrade of a steep hill and spilled all the passengers along the highway. Victor was picked up by an ambulance with a dangerous compound fracture of his left leg. A few days later a crisis set in and his life was in the balance.

After five months in a hospital, with forty others in the same ward, lying on his back in one position, leg in a cast, he finally was dismissed on crutches. Lydia at that time was going through "the depths" with her beloved brother in England, but looking to the Lord to definitely heal him. And Victor was in a Cracow hospital threatened with the amputation of one leg. Thus the Lord teaches us to keep humble and close to Him. When we think we are "sitting on top of the world," He whispers to us to come sit by Him and learn patience and longsuffering. Through it all He draws us closer to Himself.

Meantime the clouds in Europe were black and ominous. The persecution of the Jews was proceeding according to plan. By this time Lydia had worked up a lucrative business for her employer in England and a substantial export business. From eight in the morning till midnight, she could be found working in the office. But the work and the burden of her brother's illness weighed her down. She asked the

Lord what she should do. And then it seemed that He spoke to her in a very definite way.

By the spring of 1937 Jack was well on the way to a good recovery. Now Lydia felt an urge to see Victor Buksbazen after his recent accident and to discuss their future. He was anxious for her to live in Poland, and she was just as anxious not to do so. There were a number of reasons for this. Knowing the political situation and especially the plight of the Jews of Europe under Hitler, Lydia felt as if a strong hand was holding her back and warning her against living in Poland.

What then? How could two people be together and yet not live in the same country? But the Lord had laid His own plans for the future of His children. The pattern was taking shape. Oh, how unsearchable are His ways and past finding out! At the time when Lydia was visiting Cracow, that same week the General Secretary of the British Jews Society, under whom Victor Buksbazen was working in Cracow, was making his bi-annual visit to Poland. And so it was that the problem was put to him. After praying together about the situation, he decided that it would be wise at that time to call Victor Buksbazen to deputation work in Britain.

By August of 1937, Lydia and Victor were engaged to be married. As if by a miracle and against his own will Victor Buksbazen was snatched from the fury of Hitler's gas chambers and horror camps, in which all his relatives including his mother, sisters and dear ones perished. Today we know the Lord had a greater task for him to do in the United States of America.

The marriage on December 21, 1937 of Victor and Lydia in St. Colomba Presbyterian Church, Walthamstow, of which Ernest, her brother, was pastor, was a memorable occasion. By this time Jack had recovered so wonderfully that at his request he escorted the bride to the altar.

Even Mr. Silber, who was overjoyed at not losing his business manager, came to the church and to the reception. Churches in England are not heated and consequently he caught cold and lay abed with pneumonia for weeks, but he always said that he never regretted attending, as he was deeply impressed by the simple Christian ceremony.

Victor's work now consisted in preaching on behalf of the Jewish Missionary work in the various churches in England, Wales and Ireland. Soon after his marriage he started on a preaching tour which kept him away three weeks. Lydia, therefore was able to continue in her work. They lived near the well-known Hampstead Heath in London. On evenings when Victor was home, they would ramble over the Heath, taking long walks to romantic and picturesque old spots around Hampstead.

## The Witches' Night

In February 1938 Lydia was suddenly called upon to make a business trip to Germany to serve two of the largest Australian buyers of German fabrics. As she could speak German and English fluently this was a great asset in selling goods to the customers from England and overseas who could not speak German. Thus she found herself one dull February day in a hotel in Krefeld, Germany, where she was to meet her Australian customers and take them on to Cologne to the warehouse of her company.

But the next twenty-four hours brought to her some terrifying experiences. It was the first day and night of the traditional "Fasching" (equivalent of Mardi Gras or Carnival). All day long, while she waited and rested, people were coming and going. The excitement in the streets and cafes and the hotel lobby was rising with every hour. It was to be a "special" anti-Semitic display and every one, young and old, was going to honor Hitler that night in the way which would please him most. Lydia wisely stayed in her room, and behind drawn curtains watched the parade assemble.

She locked her room from the inside for she feared trouble. And then the "fun" started. Large torches were lighted and a grotesque procession of people intoxicated with liquor and hate propaganda, started up the street. She watched with bated breath. What was that they were carrying? She looked more intently, and then she realized the gruesomeness of the situation. Great caricatures and stuffed life-size dummies of such well-known Jews as Bernard Baruch, Sigmund Freud, Monsier Blum, Albert Einstein, and others, had been made. Their features were exaggerated in the most fantastic way: foot-long noses, huge ears, and big feet.

The effigies were being carried on long poles through the main street to the accompaniment of raucous voices of the Hitler "leaders" and the despicable anti-Semitic songs, such as the infamous Horst-Wessel song which began like this:

"When Jewish blood from the knife spurts
Things will go much better for us."

After each song, roared by multitudes of drunken people, there were great shouts of "Down with the Jews. Let's kill them all. Let's burn them all." Then huge bonfires were set in the main street at intervals of about one hundred yards, and the effigies were burned. The fires were kept going by the looted contents of Jewish homes nearby. This was "the superior race" which Hitler came to set free from the Jews.

While the drunken hordes were disporting themselves in revelry and merrymaking, the chief object of which was to revile and deride the Jews, the God of Israel looked down and saw the venom and the contempt poured out upon His people and held their deriders in derision. "He that sitteth in the heavens shall laugh: the Lord shall have them in derision. Then shall he speak unto them in his wrath, and vex them in his sore displeasure."

A little more than a year later God did speak to these people in his wrath and vexed them in his sore displeasure. Seven years later in 1945 the Reich which Hitler built and which was to endure a thousand years lay in ruins and beneath the rubble in a bunker in Berlin its evil founder—the man with the unruly strand of hair and funny mustache—Adolf Hitler.

Ten years later in 1948 the people of Germany again were celebrating their traditional "Fasching" night. But now instead of the hideous caricatures of famous Jews the crowds were carrying the life-size dummies of Hitler, Goehring and Goebbels, and of the demoniac Streicher, that arch-enemy and calumniator of the Jews. Then the effigies were burned in the streets of Cologne and in other cities of Germany.

Thus the God of Israel had the last laugh.

"And God said to Abraham: I will bless them that bless thee, and curse him that curseth thee"—Genesis 12.3.

Lydia watched behind the draperies at the window with dread and fear that she might be seen and the mob get her. Outside her door crowds of people kept milling around. There seemed to be hundreds of them, downstairs, in the halls upstairs, on the stairs themselves, all drinking and singing the vilest anti-Semitic songs she had ever heard. When she attempted to order food by phone from downstairs she was told to go down to the dining room and get it. That she could not do, for she was afraid to even show her face to such a hostile crowd. And so the nightmare as it seemed to her, wore on, and at last, exhausted from the noise and dreadful sight in the street, she fell asleep.

Early next morning she was awakened by a telephone call from the two customers she had been waiting for. They had arrived during the height of the "fun" and had gone to bed, disgusted. Soon the firm's chauffeur from Cologne arrived as arranged, and after a hurried breakfast took them to Cologne, an hour or so from Krefeld. The streets looked a shambles. That was the last parcel of goods Lydia sold in Germany, for she never wanted to set foot there again as long as Hitler ruled.

While Lydia was dealing with her customers at the warehouse, special agents of the Hitler party, of which every firm was forced to employ at least one or more, stood behind the glass partitions, watching furtively everything that went on, so as to enable them to report to headquarters.

## The Death of a Jewish Salesman

It so happened that at that time a well-liked Jewish salesman who had worked for the firm thirty years, had died a day before. Then the Nazis posted notices all over the offices and warehouses warning the "Aryan" employees that they should not go to the funeral or they would be expelled from the party and punished. This greatly infuriated some of the Gentile fellow-employees, who had worked with their Jewish colleague for the greater part of their lives and had learned to love and respect him. Thus the atmosphere was charged with fear, hate, suspicion and danger, in those bad old days of Hitler's Germany in 1938.

Her task completed, Lydia removed herself rapidly from Germany and caught the first plane back to London, where once again she breathed freely, and thanked God from the bottom of her heart for a free country. The memories of that trip to Cologne are indelibly fixed in her mind and she shudders at what might have happened to her, in spite of her British passport which at that time still commanded some respect in Germany. Soon Mr. Silber was able to produce the same quality goods in British factories and severed all ties with Germany, the country he once loved, but which dealt so treacherously and cruelly with her Jewish citizens.

## Chapter Twenty-eight

# A Giant Stalks the Earth

### Jacob's Last Journey

**B**Y CHRISTMAS of 1938 Jack had decided that his future was across the ocean in America where he was anxious to start life anew. It seemed to be God's will for him to go back. Two country churches in South Dakota gave Jack a call to be their pastor and the family prepared him for the journey. He was fitted out from top to toe with new clothing, new luggage, and just about everything he would need. Jack looked forward to a future full of promise.

But "My thoughts are not your thoughts, neither are your ways my ways, saith the Lord."

On January 6, 1939 (three months before Buksbazens' first son, John, was born) Jack sailed, full of hopes and dreams, looking forward to a new life in the Lord's work. Yet like Moses, he was shown the "Promised Land" but was not permitted to enter it.

How sad was Jack's parting from his mother to whom he was deeply attached! On leaving the boat Yente said to her eldest daughter Betty, "Somehow, I don't think I will ever see him again!" Further down the River Thames in London, Lydia and Victor, who were late in arriving, reached the boat as it entered a lock, and there had ten minutes conversation with Jack from the quay. He was happy and excited and told them he would secure a "call" for Victor from the United States, so that they too could go to that country he had learned to love.

"I am sure," he said to his brother-in-law, "the Lord has a special place of service for you in America." Little did he know of the "call" that awaited him on his arrival in the United States. Lydia too had the feeling that Jack would never see her baby.

Those days in January of 1939 went by fast. Due to winter storms, the crossing took about twelve days. On the seventeenth and eighteenth day after Jack sailed, Yente and the rest of the family were restless at not hearing of his safe arrival. On the nineteenth day, early in the morning, Yente was so ill at ease that she took the bus from her home in

Hutton Essex to Walthamstow where Ernest lived, about an hour away.

Ernest and his wife, Ella, and his sister Marie, who was visiting them, were at breakfast when the door bell rang. Ernest went to the door and a cable from Chicago was delivered to him. Hastily he opened it and read: "Jacob had appendectomy. Passed away. Shall we bury here?" It was signed by Mr. Lewek, President of the Hebrew Christian Alliance of America.

He was shocked and rooted to the spot, but he acted fast. Fearing to tell his wife and Marie too abruptly, he stuffed the cable in his pocket and hurried to London. On the way he called Lydia at the office. She had just arrived. He tried desperately hard to tell her, thinking she could bear it quietly and bravely. Halfway through she sensed the news and knew. Then all went black and she fainted away, falling off the chair.

When her co-workers revived her, Lydia spoke to Ernest again, and her mind started working with the whirling speed of one faced with a sudden catastrophe. They recalled that Jack had once mentioned to his mother, that in Chicago the Hebrew Christian Alliance had a plot of ground for the burial of Hebrew Christians in the beautiful Acacia Park Cemetery, and that he would like to be buried there. So they composed a reply cable, asking that their brother be buried in that cemetery. Then came the sad trek back home to convey to the rest of the family, as gently as possible, the message that Jack had gone to be with his Lord.

In the meantime Yente had arrived. She asked Ella whether they had any news from Jack, and what Ernest was doing in town so early in the morning! Ella answered truthfully that she did not know. So Yente was about to leave again when Lydia and Ernest arrived.

## The Faith of Yente

One look at their faces and she knew all was not well. Lydia took her gently into the house, sat her down (Ernest had smelling-salts prepared for a possible fainting reaction) and she started to tell her the contents of the telegram. Before she could say that he had passed away, Yente knew, and finished the sentence: "My dear Jack has gone to be with the Lord."

What happened after that will forever be the greatest testimony to the faith of Yente. Instead of fainting, as her children expected, she clasped her hands, got down on her knees, raised her head to Heaven and prayed, "Lord, I thank Thee for Thy wisdom. I will praise Thee at all times. Thou hast given, and Thou hast taken. Blessed be Thy Name."

It seemed that at that moment a host of angels encompassed her round about. They upheld her and gave her supernatural strength. She was calm and contained. "Come, my child," she said to Lydia, "we must think of you and of your child yet to be born. The Lord has taken our Jack away, and now He will give you a son in his place. You must take care of yourself, and I too must take care of you." Together they went to "Whitby Moor," their little bungalow home in Hutton, which was bound up with so many sweet and bitter memories. They were too grief-stricken and numbed to weep. Only later, when Benjamin, who previously received the news on the telephone, arrived home, the floodgates broke and each wept separately lest the other see. The blow aged Yente overnight. In the morning when she awoke after a fitful night, her hair had taken on a new hue, changing from partly grey to complete white.

Yet another drop of bitterness had to be added to their cup of sorrow. Next day, when the mail from the United States arrived, having been delayed by the winter storms for some days, there were postal cards from Jack with greetings to all members of the family, and a letter telling about the pleasant, though stormy, crossing to America. He intimated that he was well and happy and looking forward with glad anticipation to his new life as preacher and pastor.

Later it was established that when Jack arrived in America he stopped over in New York City to look up some old friends. Then on the way to his pastorate in South Dakota, he visited also in Chicago. He spent the evening at the home of one of his dear Hebrew Christian friends where they entertained him for supper. Later he returned for the night to the Y.M.C.A. But suddenly he was taken ill with an attack of appendicitis. The details of his sickness never became quite clear to his family. It seems that Jack, taken seriously ill during the night, was unable to notify others about his condition, and when finally the doctor arrived, he thought that Jack was merely suffering with acute indigestion. But when his condition changed for the worse, he was rushed to the hospital. An emergency operation for appendicitis was performed at once. However, by this time peritonitis had set in. And to complicate matters further, post-operative pneumonia developed.

Feeling that the Lord was going to take him home, Jack called together the brethren for prayer and asked to be anointed. He led in the prayer meeting himself, sitting up in the oxygen tent. All the brethren marveled at the testimony of the dying young man. He thanked God for a believing father and mother, who brought him up in the fear and the love of the Lord Jesus Christ. He committed them and all his family and the brethren to his Saviour, and fell asleep.

## Darkening Days

Anyone who did not live in Europe during those dark days in the latter part of "the terrible thirties," cannot possibly understand the sense of impending doom which hung heavily over the spirits of men. It was as if an evil giant was stalking the earth, gobbling up whole nations along the path. With each meal he seemed to grow stronger and his appetite more voracious. "Whose turn will it be next to become fodder for the giant?" nations small and large were asking themselves. The Jews who were the special object of Hitler's mad obsession were living in a kind of frenzied nightmare, as when you dream about some wrathful strong man running after you, but your feet are rooted to the spot and all escape seems barred. Only this was no dream. This nightmare was gruesomely real.

## Like Sheep to the Slaughter

The Hebrew Christian family of David Fogel, who had lived in Germany for nearly half a century, was now trapped behind those barred doors. One of their sons, Emil, made his way to Palestine. With his bare fingers and without any money, he worked hard until he was able to send for his wife and children. But his father, David Fogel, his tiny mother with a great spirit, and his two sisters, were trapped beyond escape.

The Sitenhofs in England made frantic efforts to rescue their relatives, the Fogels, but red tape enmeshed them more effectively than iron chains could possibly do. By the time permission was granted to the Fogels to come to England, war had broken out. Soon after, the Fogels were imprisoned by the Nazis and then perished in a cattle truck which was taking them to a concentration camp. But they had a hymn on their lips. A Christian lady, a friend of the Fogel family, who witnessed their departure, wrote to the Sitenhofs after the war, the sad details of their last hours.

Traveling back to her home in a passenger section for Germans, to which were hooked the cattle trucks filled with Jews, she alighted at her station, when the strains of a familiar hymn greeted her ears. She walked quickly toward the cattle trucks, hoping to get a last glimpse of the Fogel family, but instead she heard their clear voices above the wailing and moaning of the other doomed Jews, singing:

So nimm Du meine Haende und fuehre mich
Bis an mein Lebens Ende und ewiglich.
Ich kann allein nicht gehen, nicht einen Schritt,
Wo Du wirst gehen und stehen, da gehe ich mit.

So take my hands, dear Lord, and lead me on
Until my life is ended and then beyond.
I cannot walk alone, dear Lord, not one small step,
Wherever Thou goest or stayest, I will go with Thee.

Thus David and his wife Dora, and Hedwig their daughter, went joyfully home to be with the Lord. The other daughter, Martha, who was married to a devout German Christian, survived, but not without experiencing all the horrors of being persecuted and hunted like a wild animal until the end of the war.

## Trapped in Poland

Victor Buksbazen had a mother and two sisters still living in Poland. As the eldest son, he was the main support of his family since the death of his father in 1920. His sister Hanna was married to a printer and they had a sweet little boy, Abraham, who before the outbreak of the war was about four years old. His nineteen-year-old sister Dora was a student at the Warsaw Polytechnic. Sensing the approach of the war, Victor and Lydia tried their utmost to rescue at least this young promising life. Christian friends in England gave her an affidavit and enrolled her as a student at the

Reading University in England, but Dora too became entangled in red tape, and before a passport was granted, war came. Neither Victor's mother nor his sisters and their families escaped. All perished under Hitler, or in Russia while seeking to escape.

## Munich

The stronger Hitler grew, the more contemptuous he became of men and the decent opinions of the civilized world. He and Goebbels were heard over the radio frantically proclaiming their threats against the Jews, and the "rotten democracies." His henchmen and followers, drunk with power, shouted "Today Germany belongs to us, tomorrow the whole world." And the world trembled.

For years Hitler had been arming, preferring guns to butter, while the peace-craving nations were weak and disarmed. They wanted peace at all costs. In a last desperate attempt the Prime Minister of England, Neville Chamberlain, and the Prime Minister of France, Monsieur Daladier, went to Munich in September 1938 to meet with Hitler and his puppet dictator, Mussolini. Chamberlain with his black hat and umbrella became the symbol of appeasement. They begged for peace. Hitler generously promised to give them peace, if they would let him gobble up the Sudetenland, a vital section of Czechoslovakia, partially populated by people of German origin. That was all he wanted. That, and then peace! Hitler obtained what he wanted.

A few hours later Neville Chamberlain alighted from his plane in London, waving triumphantly a piece of paper signed by the Fuehrer, and announced to a jubilant crowd who came to greet him at the airport:

"I have brought peace for our time." These words will never stop ringing in the writer's ears.

Yet six months later Hitler marched into what was left of Czechoslovakia, and strutting through the streets of Prague, proclaimed himself protector of that helpless horror-stricken country. The stunned Czech people stood in the streets of Prague crying unashamedly, their freedom murdered. "Peace for our time" lasted less than six months.

Soon after, Hitler again made it known that his patience was exhausted, and unless Poland surrendered Danzig and her Baltic province, he would have to march.

It was then, that England awoke! The word "appeasement" became dishonorable.

Realizing that no plea nor any abject effort of appeasement would stop Hitler, they started arming frantically, seeking at the same time an alliance with Russia against a common foe. But Stalin, to the amazement of the world, suddenly announced that he had concluded a non-aggression pact with Hitler.

On September 1, 1939, the German Wehrmacht swooped down on the borders of Poland, her Panzer divisions and the Luftwaffe raining fire and death upon the peaceful villages and towns of Poland. After a heroic but brief resistance, Poland succumbed. On the third of September, Great Britain declared herself at war with Germany. France followed suit.

Europe was aflame. England, expecting the worst, was preparing to live underground in dugouts, known as Anderson shelters. These were provided by the Government for the protection of the civil population against air raids. For a time it was comparatively peaceful in England. People began to talk about a phony war. Yet a devastating and cruel war was being waged in Eastern Europe. After Poland was vanquished, suddenly without any warning, neutral Norway was invaded by the Nazi armies. Hitler was now master in Eastern Europe, and could turn his attention to the west.

The "phony war" took on a grim and foreboding aspect for the people of Britain. There were at that time in Britain thousands of Jewish refugees who had barely managed to escape annihilation on the European Continent. These people were particularly perplexed and apprehensive. Would their terrible enemy reach out his deadly hand and destroy them even here in England where they had found friends and protection?

Many of these people sorely in need of reassurance and comfort would gather in the homes of the Sitenhofs and Buksbazens. Those who came fearful and depressed would go away encouraged, their fears dispelled and their spirits directed toward the God of Israel who loved them and gave His all to them and for them.

Perturbed and anxious, their hearts were now open to the Word of God and to the Gospel as they had never been before. Even as the breath of life, they needed faith and where else could they find it but in the Book of Life and victorious faith. Those were days when men had to live by faith, if they were to live at all.

## Chapter Twenty-nine

# Yente Finds the City

### The Miracle of Dunkirk

NOW that Poland lay prostrate and defeated, and Norway was securely in their grip after a treacherous attack, the Nazis in the spring of 1940 turned against the Western Allies. Again, without warning they invaded neutral Holland and Belgium. After a brief battle, King Leopold II of Belgium promptly surrendered himself and his army to the Germans. The back door, in fact the whole rear wall of France, stood wide open to the invader. The vaunted Maginot Line was pitifully useless against an enemy coming from the rear. The British expeditionary forces in Europe, together with the remnants of the French, Belgian and Dutch forces, were forced to retreat toward the Channel ports of France and Belgium.

Early in June of 1940 some 330,000 soldiers, almost the entire British army, and some remnants of her Allies, found themselves trapped on the beaches of Dunkirk with their backs to the sea, and encircled by a relentless and confident enemy. One of the most nightmarish and decisive weeks in history ensued.

These men on the beaches of Dunkirk were the flower of British manhood. If they should fall into the hands of their enemies, then Britain would be at the mercy of the invaders. In a valiant effort to rescue these soldiers, all ferries, transport ships, sporting yachts, and fishing smacks, in fact, anything that could float and take a few men aboard, were rushed to the beaches of Dunkirk.

The world held its breath. Would this be the end of Britain and of freedom in Europe? A mighty stream of prayer went up to God from countless hearts everywhere. Freedom hung in the quivering balance. But the fervent prayers of many were heard and answered. The English Channel, at this time of the year usually choppy and boisterous, was strangely becalmed. Even the smallest vessels were able to make the trip and bring home some soldiers from the beaches. Some of the frail boats managed to cross the Channel several times. Most of the men, about 270,000 in all, were taken off the beaches of Dunkirk and brought home safely. However their equipment and all their arms fell into enemy hands.

## The "Sea Lion" in his Lair

While these things were taking place, Yente sat glued to the radio, waiting for every word which came across the waves concerning the turn of events. She neither ate nor drank, but fasted and prayed. She fought for her adopted homeland, with the only weapons she had—prayer and faith.

At last a kindly neighbor, seeing Yente's haggard face, brought her tea and biscuits, confidently trusting in the comforting and sustaining virtues of the proverbial British "cup o' tea." "My dear," she would coax Yente, "drink this, it will do you good." It always did!

By the middle of June 1940, the Miracle of Dunkirk was already history. England had her strong sons home again. But with her allies vanquished, Britain stood almost alone and unarmed, facing a deadly enemy, drunk with victory. Her main defense was faith, courage and hope. In the words of her towering leader, Winston Churchill, this was one of the finest hours in England's long history.

The British fully expected that the Nazis would follow up Dunkirk with an invasion of their country. Indeed the Germans were gathering an invasion fleet in the Channel Ports of Europe and mustering their mighty armies for the final blow against Britain. This they dubbed operation "Sea Lion." But "The Sea Lion," roaring defiantly, was preparing to defend himself to the last, against all odds. Great roadblocks of solid concrete were set up on highways, in fields and meadows.

## The Battle of Britain

Lydia and Victor had in the meantime given up their apartment and planned to move in with Ernest. Soon after war broke out, the American authorities anticipating heavy air raids in Britain, persuaded all United States citizens to go home while transportation was still available. Ernest's wife, Ella, for the sake of their six-months-old baby David, went back home to her parents in California.

In May 1940, Marie too had a son, Harold, but all did not go well for her and her little family. Her husband, who suffered with heart trouble, suddenly collapsed and died when the baby was two months old. Marie was so grief-stricken that she and the baby had to be hospitalized in a private nursing home. The funeral was on August 10th, and Yente was too shocked to attend. That day she had a dizzy spell in her garden and fell headlong into a six-foot ditch.

The following Monday, August 12th, on Lydia's birthday, not hearing anything definite from her mother about her condition, other than that she did not feel well, she hastened to Hutton, only to find that Yente had had a stroke and was in bed alone in the house. Benjamin, notified, came at once, but as she needed careful nursing, it was decided to transport her by ambulance to a nursing home in London, in the community where Ernest lived and where Marie was being cared for with the baby. Thus Lydia could look after them both.

It was on that day that the battle of Britain began in earnest. Great swarms of German bombers came roaring from across the Channel and darkened the skies. Their sinister heavy drone filled every heart with grim foreboding. Soon the shrill sounds of warning sirens were heard across the vast expanse of London.

That ride with Yente in the ambulance to the nursing home was a nightmare. As they started out, the shrill ear-piercing air raid warning sounded. Then the roar of the enemy planes was heard. But the ambulance proceeded until the nursing home was reached.

Day after day the enemy planes kept coming in full force, sometimes more than a thousand at a time. But the British airmen, reinforced by allied pilots who escaped to England, were able to destroy hundreds of planes time and again. It was not unusual to see dog fights taking place in the skies right over London and the suburbs, with the pilots bailing out to be killed or captured.

The man whom God raised up for that hour of grave peril to steel the will of his people for the defense of their country, Winston Churchill, said this about the men of the Royal Air Force: "Seldom in the field of human conflict have so many owed so much to so few." These knights of the air helped to turn the tide of events and to say to the tyrant: "It shall not be."

Later when the "Luftwaffe" realized that they could not bomb London into submission in daylight, they started their raids after sunset and continued their work of destruction through the night. The hordes of enemy planes would come as regularly as clockwork, and drop their load of heavy bombs or incendiary missiles, which shattered and burned whole sections of London, killing and maiming thousands.

At dusk, as soon as the sirens were sounded, or even before, people would rush to take shelter in places especially prepared for the public. Others would go to the "Anderson shelters" in their own back yards. There, together with their young children and babies, they would huddle together in the dark and dank quarters, trying to make themselves as comfortable as possible with blankets and hot water bottles. These shelters had been built with the duration of air raids in the First World War in mind, that is, that an air raid would last no longer than two or three hours.

In 1940, however, they generally lasted from 4 o'clock in the afternoon until 8 o'clock in the morning, which meant that somehow, cramped as they were, sleeping accommodations had to be arranged, at least for the children. Bunks, often no wider than 15 inches, were rigged up hurriedly. There you could stretch your weary body at least during part of the fourteen hours which it might be necessary to spend in the damp shelter.

Some would play games or talk and others sing hymns or pray. London became a city of cave dwellers. What nerve-wracking nights they were, with the constant blast of falling bombs, and the answering fire of anti-aircraft guns, and the crackle of burning timbers. The skies were illumined and crisscrossed by innumerable searchlights. London was ablaze.

In the morning, when at last the "all-clear" signal sounded, they would emerge, with the night dampness and chill in their bones, grimy, red-eyed and tired. The first concern was always to see whether your home was still standing. No one who has not been through it can appreciate the feeling of thanksgiving in people's hearts when they saw their homesteads were still intact. But many coming back from their shelters found their homes burned or blasted. Sometimes the electricity, the gas or water mains would be damaged, and no hot meals could be prepared. When the water reservoirs were hit, the misery became even more acute.

But London, determined to survive, carried on with a grim kind of humor, courageous and defiant. Men and nations are tested in days of trial and supreme peril. It is then that the true nature and inherent strength of those so tested become evident. Britain stood her test and passed it nobly.

London and outlying sections on the Thames Estuary were bombed daily. Thousands of homes and buildings, churches and hospitals went up in flames. Every night men, women and children were killed by enemy bombs or injured by fragments of anti-aircraft shells. Ghostlike streets were gutted and lifeless. Survivors were removed to less dangerous parts of the country.

Ernest, who was an air raid warden and a chaplain apart from his church pastorate, conducted many funerals of victims daily. Sometimes whole families were wiped out.

At first the noise and blast were terrifying. Children screamed in terror. Lydia had her hands full. She would make up "beds" in the shelter during the day to run there whenever necessary. As soon as "black-out" time came she would rush baby John out all dressed in a "siren" suit and try to get him to sleep before the exploding bombs became too noisy. Some of the first words the little boy learned were "black-out" and "bomb."

Yente in the nursing home was very sick indeed. The bombing worried her, so her ears were plugged, but she could still hear the noise. The patients able to walk alone to the basement shelter were encouraged to do so. But by that time Yente could not stand on her feet and her speech was impaired.

After a few days Marie and her poorly nourished infant left the nursing home and joined Lydia's household. But Marie was not herself and was too grief-stricken to even look after her son. Every morning with John in the pram, Lydia would take chicken broth to the nursing home for her mother. But she noticed that her condition was getting worse. Yente begged to be brought to Ernest's house, as she could not stay on the third floor of the nursing home during those dreadful raids which lasted for eight hours or more, and then through the night!

What confusion and chaos everywhere!!

Victor's activities in the meantime on behalf of "The British Jews Society" were of necessity being curtailed. As a "friendly alien" (Polish) he could travel freely in so-called non-defense areas, but the whole coastline was declared a "defense area." This meant that he could not go to many of the churches who had invited him to speak weeks before anything like this was anticipated. Nor was it possible to visit the heavily bombed and burned out East End of London, where so many of the Jewish people lived.

At that time the Lord laid it upon the heart of a Missionary Society in America to give him a call, which he accepted gladly, although it seemed quite obscure when the time would come that the Buksbazens would get their visas and secure transportation to America across the submarine-infested Atlantic. But in this too Victor and Lydia experienced the truth, that with God all things are possible.

Events followed each other swiftly in the late autumn of 1940. Daylight was so short, that in retrospect one has to marvel how the Lord enabled Lydia to do all the things that were needed: to feed, wash and comfort two babies, look after a household, two men, and above all, her sick mother in the nursing home, and to comfort a grief-stricken sister in her bereavement. All this while London was experiencing the worst air raids up to that time. Those were days to try the hearts even of the strongest. Blessed was the person whose heart was stayed upon Jehovah.

"God is our refuge and strength, a very present help in trouble. Therefore will not we fear!"—Psalm 46:1,2.

## Yente Finds the City

Yente was not improving. How could she? She needed peace and quiet to survive a stroke such as she had had. Instead there was the explosion of bombs, and the wailing of air raid sirens. To make things worse, medical aid was hard to obtain, as nurses and doctors alike were evacuated from London at the beginning of the bombing, or were in military service.

Yente was dying and she knew it. So she begged to go back to her beloved Whitby Moor in Hutton. Unfortunately it was a "defense area" where large anti-aircraft guns paraded up and down, and shot at the planes as they came from the Continent, to prevent them from reaching the heart of London. The blast from the anti-aircraft firing was often more terrifying than the bombs themselves.

Lydia went back to Hutton with her mother and the baby in an ambulance which had a large Red Cross on the roof, and tried to nurse her as best she could, although she had no experience at all. Victor and Ernest stayed in Walthamstow where Ernest had his church, only half of which by now was standing. Large sheets of tarpaulin covered the gaping holes of the church where walls had been, and the services were conducted sometimes under a blue sky, as the roof was badly damaged. Those were grim days indeed!

By the end of August the strain was too much for Lydia. Betty and her husband who were keeping house in the country for a farmer, relieved her for a week or two, and then she continued with a broken heart to nurse the mother she loved so dearly. Yente's swallowing muscles had become paralyzed and she was getting weaker daily. She had to be tied down in bed with sheets during the terrible night raids as the blast could have blown her out of bed. The agony of seeing her suffer was so great for the family, added to the abnormal air raid conditions, that sometimes Lydia prayed, "Oh Lord, let this not continue—give her peace and rest!"

At last an elderly nurse was found and a small thatched cottage rented deep in the country, where the doctor said she might stand a chance to recover, if she got away from the actual bombing area and big guns. Benjamin too went along.

Again the ambulance arrived. They carried her gently on the stretcher. And then the wailing of the sirens started. "Never mind," she said as she kissed her child, "there is rest and peace with the Lord and I am going to Him." She was losing ground steadily. Her paralyzed throat muscles did not permit her to receive nourishment. A few days later Yente went into a coma. Seven weeks of starvation were more than her frail body could endure.

Then the Lord swung open the gates of Heaven to His journey-worn handmaiden. The Pilgrim was home! At last Yente entered the City of her longings and her prayers, "The City which hath foundations, whose builder and maker is God."